Kevin Belton

Kevin Belton's

COOKIN'
LOUISIANA

Kevin Belton's
COOKIN' LOUISIANA

FLAVORS FROM THE PARISHES OF THE PELICAN STATE

KEVIN BELTON
WITH **MONICA BELTON**

Photographs by Denny Culbert

GIBBS SMITH
TO ENRICH AND INSPIRE HUMANKIND

First Edition
25 24 23 22 21   5 4 3 2

Text © 2021 Kevin Belton
Photographs © 2021 Denny Culbert

Published by
Gibbs Smith
P.O. Box 667
Layton, Utah 84041

1.800.835.4993 orders
www.gibbs-smith.com

Front cover designed by Ryan Thomann
Designed by Dawn DeVries Sokol
Printed and bound in China
Gibbs Smith books are printed on either recycled, 100% post-consumer waste, FSC-certified papers or on paper produced from sustainable PEFC-certified forest/controlled wood source. Learn more at www.pefc.org.

Library of Congress Control Number: 2021930992
ISBN: 978-1-4236-5838-2

To my wife, my family, and all Louisianians—from the state and from the heart.
— KEVIN BELTON

To Noah, Kevin, and Cookie Monster. You are my whole world and I love you with all my heart.
— MONICA BELTON

CONTENTS

ACKNOWLEDGMENTS

Creating a cookbook is an all-encompassing culinary journey that I love, but need so much help navigating. I am fortunate to have so many people helping me every step along the way. First is my wife Monica, y'all know she does it all, and then my family, who is always there to offer support and information.

Denny Culbert, for making something that tastes so good, look so great. To Michelle Branson and the Gibbs Smith team for offering incredibly wonderful support, and for helping us put our work into something tangible that you can hold.

To Maura Kye-Casella from Don Congdon Associates for helping us every step along the way, and leading us down the yellow brick road.

Lenny and Joanie Delbert for becoming family, and to Lenny for being a fishing buddy, confidante, photographer, videographer, editor, and partner in crime.

To all of Louisiana—Louisiana has a certain feel, a look, a sound, a smell, and a taste. And Louisiana has a heartbeat, a heartbeat that all Louisianians contribute to. It is a heartbeat unlike any other that goes on and on. More importantly, Louisiana is love. Love that we all want to share with everyone.

I want to thank everyone who takes this culinary journey with us. I strive every day to have fun and share my experiences with food. It always feels better to go through this wild and wonderful culinary journey with friends.

Da Crew

As the television host of *Kevin Belton's Cookin' Louisiana* from WYES-TV studios, it makes sense that you see me, but I always wish you could see everyone on the crew. Every person listed below worked incredibly hard to make the show a success. They are all talented and wonderful people who have become family. This may sound crazy, but it takes all of these people to make me look so good, and the show would not be the same without them. I wanted to you to see them and read a few things about them, so they became as real to you as they are to me.

President and CEO of WYES-TV Allan Pizzato
Vice President and COO of WYES-TV Robin Cooper
Executive Producer Jim Moriarty is Irish, and that says a lot, but he's also a wonderful person and a great friend. He has the ability of seeing talent in people, putting those people in the right positions, and letting them do their jobs.
Producer/Director Terri Landry is a talented and tough producer. She has a vision for something and goes after it. We often have the same vision and direction, and it's weird, because we wonder if we have said things out loud, but we haven't, we are just thinking the same thing.
Associate Producer Dawn Smith gets things done, and I love having her in my corner. Dawn and her husband Allan have become great friends. She and Monica often plot and plan, but the end result is to make me look good.
Production Coordinator Darlene Kennedy makes things happen, and she is one of the sweetest people you could ever know.

Technical Director Laura Combel works the switcher, switching between cameras for the line cut. Laura also makes sure the cameras are in focus and lets the camera technicians know what to expect for the filming. Laura is married to Scotty and they have two cute little girls, Izzy and Remy, who also love to cook.

Video David Kennedy watches the monitors, confirms we are in legal broadcast limits, and makes adjustments as necessary when we record. Technically he is retired, but he comes back when needed, and he is also married to Darlene Kennedy.

Development and Sound Jim Tapley works in development, but since he worked in radio earlier in his career, it makes sense that he would help out with sound.

Media Operations Fred Barrett is a staple at WYES, and he can fix anything!

Camera 1 Dave Landry is married to Producer Terri, and is very good at his job. If you are looking at me on screen, he shoots my left. He also loves boudin.

Camera 2 Lonny Delbert, Sr. is an incredible cameraman, editor, fisherman, and friend. If you are looking at me on screen, he is the camera I face directly. Lenny and his wife Joanie are close family friends. He was one of the few people who helped us plan our surprise wedding. Lenny, Joanie, and their small herd of dachshunds live just a few blocks from us.

Camera 3 Rene Champagne operates the camera where I look when I'm cooking at the stove. Because I'm so tall, Rene stands on risers. Rene, Lenny Jr., and I share the same birthday.

Lighting Lenny Delbert, Jr. is the son of Lenny Sr. and they are quite the dynamic duo. Lenny Jr. typically does lighting, but he is also an excellent cameraman. Lenny Jr. was another person who helped plan our surprise wedding. We also have the same wedding anniversary, which is a good thing since we can remind each other.

Camera 3 Walter Bardell keeps his camera focused on me as I cook. I have known him for well over thirty years. I am also lucky enough to see him weekly at WWL (the CBS affiliate in New Orleans). He is in demand!

Jib Operator Scott Combel operates the jib, which is the big, high sweeping camera that catches those beautiful overhead shots. He is married to Laura Combel.

Stage Manager Kelsi Schreiber has worked on all four seasons of my show. She has done a few different jobs, but she is mostly the floor director. She is four-feet-nine-inches tall, so I am literally TWO WHOLE FEET taller than she is. There are so many incredibly funny moments with Kelsi because of our size difference, but there is no one I would rather take floor direction from.

Prompter Steven Patriquin has also worked on all of my cooking shows. He runs the teleprompter, and he loves to eat. I don't know where he puts all that food.

Makeup Ingrid Butler has worked as a makeup artist for WYES for many years, but this was the first time she worked on my show. I loved all the laughs and comic relief with her as well as all of the makeup advice.

Technical Support George Matulik makes sure things run smoothly, particularly when wires get crossed. He quickly gets them uncrossed so we can get rolling.

Prep Kitchen Chef Jay Meeuwenberg ran the prep kitchen for the show. He was my right-hand man and a great chef. Claire Holcomb and Faith Shepherd worked with Chef Jay. They brought all the beautifully prepped food out to the set, and took care of cleanup and washing dishes.

KEVIN BELTON'S
COOKIN' LOUISIANA

I have been a taste tester for as long as I can remember, and that is a long time. While I was growing up, it didn't matter if it was my grandmother, mom, or dad, they always wanted me to know flavors. It was amazing how things could look so different from how they tasted. It allowed me to realize how flavors can change as ingredients age, some good and some not so good. Flavors also change from raw to cooked, and by different methods of cooking. That's something I learned early on, try things a few times. You may not care for it one way, but when prepared a different way, the taste and texture can be totally different.

In Louisiana, we have sixty-four parishes, which are like counties in every other state. They were originally church units set up by the Spanish Provisional Governor of Louisiana. My mom's passion for cooking prompted her to get behind the wheel of the car and visit parish after parish to seek out the best ingredients for the best flavors, the fresher the better. While the farm-to-table concept is currently very popular, it was always normal for us.

As a kid, I was able to see crops growing in the soil, chickens in a coop, pigs in the pen, and cows grazing in the fields. I wish all kids could have the same opportunity at some point. When we are young, we have a natural curiosity. Bring a child to the farmer's market because not only can they see, smell, and touch freshly harvested goods, but they can ask the growers questions like. "How long does it take to grow?" "How do you know when it is ready to be picked?" "Why are there

so many different colors and textures?" For me, when I went to the grocery store, I was distracted by cereal, cookies, candy, and cakes, you know all the important things in a six-year old's life. The other aisles were boring and were for the adults. But because of my excursions with my mother, and summers spent with cousins running around farms, my eyes were opened and I had a firm understanding of where my food came from.

Southwest of New Orleans is the town of Des Allemands. It was originally settled by German immigrants who grew crops which supplied the city. On the Northshore of Lake Pontchartrain, there were also farms that grew crops and raised animals to provide the city with its bounty. Over the years some of the farms have disappeared, but many continue to this day, and there is a resurgence of new ones happening now. This is not unique to New Orleans. Take a look at cities near where you live, and with a bit of research, you will find farms that have provided, and still provide, supplies for grocers and restaurants in your area.

When most people think of Louisiana, New Orleans is what comes to mind. That may be because it is the state's largest city. But Louisiana has five regions: Greater New Orleans, River Parishes, Cajun Country, Crossroads, and Sportsman's Paradise. The regions represent the diversity of Louisiana's culture, but there are many similarities among them.

The Greater New Orleans region has a personality all its own. That's because of the variety of people first drawn centuries ago to the area for the resources and trade route provided by the Mississippi River. Native Americans, French, Spanish, Haitian, Irish, German, and many others gathered here, and their influences are still alive and well in the music, food, and architecture of the area.

In the River Parishes, the Mississippi River winds its way to the Gulf of Mexico. Historic mansions recall a time when the fertile grounds along the river delivered much wealth. Many of the homes featuring Greek Revival, Victorian, and Italianate style are still standing for those history buffs looking to explore the past.

Cajun Country offers plenty of good times, usually happening at the table over a meal, but just as often taking place at a gathering surrounded with Cajun or Zydeco music. Living among the swamps and cypress trees inspire an appreciation for the land and the culture it has provided. The joy of life is celebrated at every turn.

The Crossroads region is an area that some people like to call a gumbo because it has a mix of cultures that has been simmering for centuries. There's a bit of Spanish, French, African-American, Anglo-American, a dash of Native American, and Cajun ingenuity. This is where the cultures of North and South Louisiana collide. It's a region known for Creole architecture, annual powwows, and pork tamales. This area has also been home to well-known politicians and icons of music.

Sportsman's Paradise has year-round celebrations that focus on a culture that embraces food and fun. The sun and soil produce fantastic peaches, while the quiet waters are loaded with bream, catfish, and bass. You can hangout outdoors following a bird trail, hike the hills, canoe a peaceful lake, or take a bike path. If you're feeling lucky and want to stay inside, there are a number of casinos and a horse-racing track to keep you entertained.

I've been fortunate to crisscross Louisiana top to bottom and side to side many times over, from big cities to small, some not even on a map, just a name on a sign. Each parish is as different as is a crayon in the sixty-four-color box, all united to make Louisiana great but each one a special gem. So please join me at the table as I take you cookin' along my Louisiana. Oh yeah, you're going to need a fork.

LAFOURCHE PARISH AND LAFOURCHE CROSSING

Kevin's Family

Bayou Lafourche flows for 106 miles through Ascension, Assumption, and Lafourche parishes. The bayou is a distributary from the Mississippi River, and the surrounding area became home to the fist settlements of Acadians in South Louisiana. This began the close association of the bayou with Cajun culture.

I came to know Lafourche Parish because this is the area where my dad's family lived before moving forty-five miles to New Orleans. Although Grandmother Emily lived in New Orleans by the time I came around, I was able to watch and learn the traditions of true South Louisiana bayou life; living off of the land.

Grandma Emily cooked every day and always used the freshest ingredients available.

I've visited areas that have rolling hills, beautiful mountains, and wonderful change of seasons, including snow, which is something I have only seen here in my life maybe three times, but my soul is at peace when I can be close to a tree-lined bayou with its gumbo-colored water. Lafourche Crossing is where the Belton family firmly planted its roots, and to have an understanding of the area, is to have a better understanding of who I am. This may explain the webbing between my toes and the comfort I feel being around water.

SEAFOOD CRÊPES

MAKES 6 TO 8 SERVINGS

6 mushrooms, chopped

3 tablespoons sliced green onion

3 tablespoons butter

2 cloves garlic, minced

3½ cups cooked and chopped crawfish, crab, and shrimp

¼ cup heavy cream

4 ounces cream cheese, cubed

3 tablespoons chopped parsley

2 tablespoons Creole seasoning

½ teaspoon kosher salt

2 tablespoons sherry wine

16 crêpes

1 cup grated pepper jack cheese

¼ cup chopped green onions

Preheat oven to 350 degrees, and set out 2 (7 x 12-inch) baking dishes.

Sauté the mushrooms and sliced green onion in butter until tender; stir in garlic. Add the seafood, cream, cream cheese, and parsley to the pan, and season with Creole seasoning and salt. Cook, gently stirring over medium heat, until the cheese has melted. Stir in sherry.

In each crêpe, place ¼ cup seafood filling, roll, and place seam side down in a baking dish. Top crêpes with the pepper jack cheese and chopped green onions and place in oven until the crêpes are hot, approximately 15 minutes.

Crêpes
MAKES ABOUT 16 CRÊPES

2¼ cups all-purpose flour

¾ teaspoon kosher salt

½ teaspoon baking powder

3 eggs

3 cups milk

2 tablespoons butter, melted

Whisk flour, salt, and baking powder together in a large bowl. Mix in eggs, milk, and butter. Using a hand beater, mix until smooth.

Lightly brush an 8-inch skillet or crêpe pan with butter, and heat over medium until bubbly. Pour in ¼ cup batter and swirl it around to coat the pan. Cook until top is dry and bottom is light brown. Flip and cook the other side. Stack on top of each other on a plate and keep warm. You can make the crêpes ahead and stack them with waxed paper between each one, and refrigerate for up to 2 days or freeze for up to 3 months.

STUFFED CRABS

Makes 4 to 6 servings

1 pound crabmeat

½ pound shrimp, chopped

½ cup diced onion

½ cup diced red bell pepper

¼ cup diced celery

2 cloves garlic, minced

1 tablespoon Worcestershire sauce

1 tablespoon Creole seasoning

1 teaspoon granulated garlic

1 teaspoon minced thyme

¼ teaspoon cayenne pepper

3 tablespoons seasoned breadcrumbs, plus ½ cup more for topping

¼ cup grated Parmesan cheese, plus ½ cup more for topping

4 tablespoons mayonnaise

1½ teaspoons kosher salt

1 egg white

4 to 6 crab shells, cleaned

3 tablespoons butter, melted

Hot sauce

Lemon wedges

Preheat oven to 375 degrees and line a baking sheet with parchment paper.

In a large bowl, combine the crab, shrimp, onion, bell pepper, celery, garlic, Worcestershire sauce, Creole seasoning, granulated garlic, thyme, cayenne pepper, breadcrumbs, Parmesan cheese, mayonnaise, salt, and egg white. Gently mix the ingredients together until well combined.

Stuff the cleaned crab shells with the mixture until all is gone. Mix together the remaining breadcrumbs with the remaining Parmesan cheese and melted butter. Place about 1 tablespoon breadcrumb mixture on top of each crab. Carefully set the stuffed crabs on the baking sheet and bake for 10–15 minutes until topping is golden brown. Serve with hot sauce and lemon wedges.

LOUISIANA OYSTER STEW

Makes 4 servings

½ cup butter

½ cup thinly sliced green onions

¼ cup diced sweet onion

¼ cup diced celery

1 tablespoon Creole seasoning

¼ cup all-purpose flour

2 cups half-and-half

1 pint oysters with their liquor

Kosher salt

Hot sauce

Parsley, for garnish

In a small Dutch oven, melt butter over medium heat. Add green onions, sweet onion, celery, and Creole seasoning; cook until softened, stirring occasionally, about 10 minutes. Sprinkle with flour and cook, stirring constantly, for 5 minutes.

Stir in half-and-half and bring to a simmer. Cook, stirring often, until thickened, about 10 minutes.

Stir in oysters and liquor. Cook until oysters are cooked through, 3-5 minutes. Add salt and hot sauce to taste. Garnish with parsley.

ST. MARTIN PARISH
Crawfish Capital

Breaux Bridge has taken on the identity as being the Crawfish Capital of the World, and this title is very well deserved. On my first visit to the Crawfish Festival, my neck was sore from turning side to side so many times reading all of the different ways crawfish was being served. There was fried, boiled, étouffée, crawfish dogs and burgers, boudin, pie, bisque, sauce picante, and so many more. And as time passes, more dishes and preparations are added. I know what you are thinking, and YES, I have tasted a little bit from every booth.

The town sits on Bayou Teche where Acadian pioneer, Firmin Breaux, built a foot bridge to make it possible to cross the water. It was a landmark people used when giving directions, such as, "When you get to Breaux's Bridge . . . ," and that's how the city got its name. St. Martin Parish is also known for Henry Wadsworth Longfellow who wrote the poem *Evangeline, a Tale of Acadie*. A young girl named Emmeline Labiche was thought by many to be the historical Evangeline, and is said to be buried at St. Martin de Tours Catholic Church in St. Martinville.

STUFFED CATFISH
OVER PASTA

Makes 4 servings

4 (8-ounce) catfish fillets

2 tablespoons Creole seasoning

1 teaspoon kosher salt

1 tablespoon olive oil, plus ½ cup more

4 strips bacon, diced

¼ cup diced celery

¼ cup diced onion

3 cloves garlic, minced

½ pound crawfish, divided

2 tablespoons finely chopped parsley

4 tablespoons butter, melted

¼ cup white wine

¼ cup grated Parmesan cheese

3 to 5 quarts chicken or vegetable stock

1 pound spaghetti

8 cloves garlic, thinly sliced

½ teaspoon crushed red pepper flakes

Chopped fresh parsley and freshly-grated
   Parmesan cheese, for garnish

Preheat oven to 350 degrees.

Sprinkle fish fillets with Creole seasoning and salt. Set aside.

Heat 1 tablespoon oil in a skillet over medium-high heat. Add bacon, celery, and onion and sauté until the bacon is crisp and the vegetables are soft. Add the minced garlic and cook for 2 minutes more. Then stir in half of the crawfish.

Remove the skillet from the heat and stir in parsley. Spread the mixture over the fish fillets, roll them up, and fasten with a toothpick.

Add a little of the melted butter to a small baking dish and swirl it so that the butter coats the bottom of the dish. Add the fish rolls. Pour the remaining butter over the fish and add the wine. Sprinkle with Parmesan cheese. Bake for 30 minutes.

In a large stockpot, bring stock to a boil. Add spaghetti and cook until al dente.

About 3 minutes after you add the pasta to the boiling stock, heat the remaining oil in a large sauté pan over medium heat. Add the sliced garlic, crushed red pepper flakes, and remaining crawfish and sauté for 3–5 minutes, or until it is lightly golden.

As soon as the pasta is ready, use tongs to transfer the pasta to the sauté pan, along with ½ cup of the hot starchy pasta water. Toss the pasta continuously until it is evenly coated in the garlic sauce. If the sauce looks a bit too dry, add in another ¼ cup of the starchy pasta water.

Serve immediately on a plate. Place stuffed fish on top and sprinkle with parsley and cheese.

CRAWFISH BURGERS

Makes 6 servings

4 tablespoons butter, divided

2 tablespoons olive oil, divided

1 onion, diced

1 red bell pepper, diced

1 yellow bell pepper, diced

1 green bell pepper, diced

3 cloves garlic, minced

2 pounds crawfish tails, lightly chopped

½ cup mayonnaise

1 tablespoon Creole mustard

2 tablespoons Worcestershire sauce

1 tablespoon Creole seasoning

2 eggs, lightly beaten

½ cup grated Parmesan cheese

1½ cups seasoned breadcrumbs, divided

¼ cup all-purpose flour

6 buns

Lettuce and sliced tomato

Heat 2 tablespoons of butter and 1 tablespoon of oil in a skillet, and cook the onion, bell peppers, and garlic until tender, 5–7 minutes. Remove from heat and add to large mixing bowl.

Add the crawfish, mayonnaise, mustard, Worcestershire sauce, Creole seasoning, eggs, Parmesan cheese, and 1 cup of the breadcrumbs. Mix everything well and refrigerate for at least 4 hours and up to overnight.

When ready to fry, heat remaining butter and oil in a large skillet over medium heat. Combine the flour and remaining breadcrumbs in a shallow bowl. Form the chilled crawfish mixture into patties, about 1 inch thick. Dredge the patties in the breadcrumb mixture, coating the surface.

Gently lower the patties into the hot skillet, and cook until golden brown, 4–5 minutes per side. Serve on buns with a smear of tartar sauce, lettuce, and tomato.

Tartar Sauce

Makes about 1 cup

1 cup mayonnaise

¼ cup finely chopped dill pickles

2 green onions, chopped

1 tablespoon capers, finely chopped

1 tablespoon chopped flat-leaf parsley

1 tablespoon lemon juice

1 teaspoon Creole mustard

1 tablespoon garlic sauce

½ teaspoon hot sauce

½ teaspoon Creole seasoning

Combine all ingredients in a small bowl, and refrigerate until ready to use.

CRAWFISH SALAD WITH SPICY DRESSING

Spicy Dressing

2/3 cup olive oil

1/3 cup red wine vinegar

3 tablespoons freshly squeezed lemon juice

1/2 teaspoon kosher salt

1/2 teaspoon ground black pepper

2 cloves garlic, minced

1/4 teaspoon dry mustard

1/2 to 1 teaspoon hot sauce

1/2 teaspoon paprika

1 1/2 tablespoons sugar

1/4 teaspoon crushed basil leaves

1/2 teaspoon crushed fresh oregano

1/4 teaspoon crushed thyme

2 serrano peppers, seeds removed and minced

Crawfish Salad

Lettuce leaves, arugula, or spring mix

1 to 1 1/2 pounds crawfish tails, cooked and chilled

12 cherry tomatoes, halved

1/2 red onion, thinly sliced

1 red bell pepper, cut into thin strips

4 eggs, hard boiled and quartered

Spicy Dressing

In a blender, combine all of the dressing ingredients as listed. Bend until completely smooth. Taste and add additional salt if the dressing needs it. If it's too sour, blend in a bit of honey. Refrigerate to chill. Dressing keeps well in the refrigerator, covered, for 1–2 weeks.

Crawfish Salad

On individual salad plates, arrange lettuce, arugula, or spring mix. Place a portion of crawfish in the center of the plated greens. Arrange tomatoes halves, red onion slices, bell pepper, and egg quarters around the crawfish on each plate. Serve the salad with the chilled dressing on the side.

IBERIA PARISH
Sugar Cane Country

When I was young, I always knew the holidays were near when I would see sugar cane laying on side of the road having fallen off the cane wagons. I can still taste the first piece of sugar cane my dad peeled and cut for me, telling me to chew on it to get the sugar out. Mom always had a stalk or two in the kitchen to use in different ways. I also remember trying to play hide and seek in a sugar cane field, which is harder than you could ever imagine. Corn grows in rows and you can walk through those rows, but sugar cane weaves itself with its neighboring rows, making it pretty much impossible to walk through or hide in.

Recently, I was lucky enough to tour a sugar cane farm, and climbed up into a combine. It was fascinating riding through the rows and harvesting the sugar cane. Having grown up in Louisiana, it was a dream come true. Iberia is part of the Sugar Parishes and produces the most sugar cane of any parish in all of Louisiana. Iberia is a sweet place, and it is also the home of three of the five salt domes of Louisiana, Jefferson Island, Avery Island, and Weeks Island. I guess you can say Iberia Parish is salty and sweet.

SUGAR CANE SHRIMP

Makes 8 servings

1½ pounds shrimp

1 teaspoon Creole seasoning

½ tablespoon chicken bouillon powder

1 tablespoon fish sauce

½ teaspoon kosher salt

2 teaspoons sugar

1 tablespoon cooking oil

4 cloves garlic, finely chopped

3 red shallots, finely chopped

1 green onion, finely chopped

1 tablespoon minced lemongrass

1 chile pepper, finely chopped

½ pound Pork Paste

1½ teaspoons cornstarch

½ teaspoon baking soda

1 cup all-purpose flour

8 sugar cane sticks

2 egg yolks

Cooking oil for frying

Banana leaves for steaming

Mint, Thai basil, bean sprouts, jalapeño, lime wedges, and cilantro, for serving

Rice noodles, cooked

Place the shrimp on a cloth to dry and pat the moisture away using paper towels.

Put the shrimp in a ziplock bag along with the Creole seasoning, bouillon powder, fish sauce, salt, and sugar. Use a meat mallet to pound the shrimp for 3 minutes then set aside.

Heat a pan with 1 tablespoon oil and brown the garlic, shallots, green onion, lemongrass, and chile.

In a food processor, add the fried aromatics, shrimp, and Pork Paste along with the cornstarch and baking soda then purée the contents until it forms a smooth paste. Put paste into a bowl and add flour. Combine until fully incorporated.

Wrap about ½ cup paste around each sugar cane stick. Wearing gloves and coating them in a light layer of oil will stop the mixture from sticking to your hands. To make the surface smooth, roll the sugar cane in the palm of your hand.

Set up a steamer on high heat, line bottom of each level with 1 banana leaf, place each sugar cane skewer on a banana leaf on tray, and steam for 5 minutes or until cooked.

Turn off the heat then lightly brush egg yolks on each steamed skewer and let it rest in the steamer for 1 minute. This step will allow the yolk to form a glaze over the meat without overcooking.

Preheat the oil in a deep fryer or a cast iron skillet to 350 degrees. Deep fry the skewers for 5–10 minutes or until golden brown. Serve immediately with fresh herbs and rice noodles. While you don't eat the sugar cane skewer, you can chew on it to get the sweetness out of it.

Pork Paste

MAKES ABOUT 1 POUND

1 pound ground pork

½ tablespoon baking powder

1 tablespoon cornstarch

2 teaspoons sugar

1½ tablespoons vegetable oil

1 tablespoon fish sauce

Add all ingredients into a food processor. Pulse and occasionally scrape down the sides with a rubber spatula. Grind until well mixed. Can be refrigerated for up to 3 days, or frozen for 2 months.

SHORT RIBS ON POTATO WAFFLES

MAKES 4 TO 6 SERVINGS

2 tablespoons vegetable oil

5 pounds bone-in short ribs, at least 1½ inches thick

Kosher salt and freshly ground pepper

2 heads garlic, halved crosswise

1 onion, chopped

1 cup chopped celery

2 carrots, sliced

2 tablespoons Creole seasoning

3 tablespoons tomato paste

¼ cup cane syrup

2 cups dry red wine

2 cups beef stock, plus more as needed

4 sprigs thyme

1 cup coarsely chopped parsley

½ cup finely chopped chives

1 lemon, zested

Sour cream

Chopped green onions

Extra cane syrup, for drizzle

Preheat oven to 275 degrees. Heat oil in a large Dutch oven over medium-high heat. Season short ribs on all sides with salt and pepper. Working in batches, sear short ribs on all sides until deeply and evenly browned, 6–8 minutes per batch. Transfer browned short ribs to a large plate and continue with remaining ribs.

Pour off all but 2 tablespoons of remaining fat, leaving the browned bits behind. Reduce heat to medium, and add garlic, cut side down and cook, until golden brown, 1–2 minutes. Add onion, celery, and carrots and season with Creole seasoning. Toss to coat and continue to cook until vegetables are softened, 5–10 minutes. Add tomato paste and stir to coat. Continue to cook, stirring occasionally, until tomato paste has started to caramelize, 2–3 minutes.

Add cane syrup and red wine, and using a wooden spoon, scrape up any browned or caramelized bits. Let this simmer 2–3 minutes. Stir in beef stock along with thyme. Return short ribs to the pot, along with any juices that have accumulated, making sure that they are submerged. If they are just barely covered, place them bone side up so that all the meat is submerged, adding more beef stock as necessary to cover. Bring to a simmer then cover and transfer to oven.

Cook until short ribs are tender and can be shredded with a fork, 3½–4 hours.

Remove the ribs from the pot, taking care not to let the bone slip out, and transfer to a large plate. Scatter parsley, chives, and lemon zest over the top of the short ribs. Separate the fat from the sauce, season with salt and pepper and serve on the side. Serve short ribs on top of potato waffles with sour cream, chopped green onions, and drizzled with cane syrup.

Potato Waffles

MAKES 3 WAFFLES (DOUBLE THIS RECIPE TO GO WITH THE SHORT RIBS)

2 tablespoons vegetable oil

¼ cup buttermilk

2 eggs

2½ cups mashed potatoes

¼ cup chopped green onions

1 cup grated cheddar cheese

½ cup all-purpose flour

½ teaspoon baking powder

¼ teaspoon baking soda

Sour cream, for serving

Preheat waffle iron and prepare with nonstick cooking spray.

In large bowl, whisk together oil, buttermilk, and eggs. Stir in the mashed potatoes, green onions, and cheese until well combined.

In a separate small bowl, whisk together the flour, baking powder, and baking soda. Fold the flour mixture into the potato mixture until it's well combined. Scoop ½ to ⅔ cup of the mixture into the prepared waffle iron, spreading it into an even layer. The potato mixture will not spread or expand as much as a regular waffle, so it's important to spread it in an even layer. Close the lid and let the waffle bake until golden brown and the egg is cooked throughout. Transfer the waffle to a serving plate then repeat the baking process with the remaining potato mixture.

CANE SYRUP CAKE

2 ½ cups all-purpose flour

1 teaspoon cinnamon

1 teaspoon ground ginger

½ teaspoon ground cloves

½ teaspoon kosher salt

½ cup vegetable oil

1 ½ cups Steen's cane syrup

1 egg

1 ½ teaspoons baking soda

¾ cup hot water

Cane Syrup Frosting

½ cup butter, softened

4 cups powdered sugar

2 teaspoons vanilla extract

½ teaspoons kosher salt

4 tablespoons Steen's cane syrup

Preheat oven to 350 degrees. Grease and flour 1 (9-inch) round cake pan.

In a bowl, combine the flour, cinnamon, ginger, cloves, and salt. Stir to mix well. In a separate bowl, combine the oil, cane syrup, and egg. Whisk to combine well.

Add about ⅓ of the flour mixture to the syrup mixture and then stir gently, just until the flour disappears. Add the baking soda to the hot water and then stir about half the water into the batter. Stir in another ⅓ of the flour mixture, then the remaining water, and finally the remaining flour, stirring gently each time just to mix everything well.

Quickly pour the batter into the prepared pan, and bake for 30–35 minutes, until the cake springs back when touched gently in the center, and is beginning to pull away from the sides of the pan. Cool the cake in the pan on a wire rack for 15 minutes. Then turn it out of the pan and place it, top side up, on the wire rack to cool completely.

Cane Syrup Frosting

In a bowl, beat the butter until light and fluffy. Add in half the powdered sugar, the vanilla, and salt. Beat at medium speed until smooth. Add the remaining powdered sugar and the cane syrup and beat until smooth and creamy, periodically scraping down the bowl.

Place cooled cake on a serving plate or cake stand, top side down, and generously spread the frosting over it, covering the top and sides.

LAFAYETTE PARISH
Epicenter of Cajun Cuisine

Famous for its hospitality and vitality of Cajun culture, Lafayette Parish has some of the best food on the planet. It also hosts two incredible events, the Festival International de Louisiane, an annual music and arts festival celebrating the French heritage of the region, and the Festival Acadiens et Creoles, a three-day festival honoring the Cajun and Creole culture.

I attended Louisiana State University (LSU), but my sons Kevin and Jonathon decided to dive head first into Cajun culture when they enrolled at the University of Louisiana at Lafayette (ULL). It was only a matter of time before they were making weekly trips throughout the parish to meat markets, getting smoked sausage, andouille, crackling, boudin, and countless other Cajun goodies. They also discovered that some of the best plates and sandwiches weren't in restaurants, but rather were acquired from small family-run stores and gas stations. Yes, we often planned our driving routes based on lunch and dinner. In choosing to enroll at ULL, they were exposed to the French culture I experienced growing up with French speaking grandparents. I know it is a few years away, but if our youngest son decides to attend Tulane University, we will have a sweet triple play of Louisiana universities.

DOWN-THE-BAYOU HOT SOFT-SHELL CRABS

MAKES 4 SERVINGS

Cooking oil for frying

¼ cup milk

3 eggs

1 tablespoon Louisiana-style hot sauce

1 cup all-purpose flour

1 cup cornstarch

1 tablespoon Creole seasoning

2 teaspoons kosher salt

4 soft-shell crabs, cleaned

½ cup butter

1 tablespoon Worcestershire sauce

1 tablespoon cayenne pepper

3 tablespoons brown sugar

½ teaspoon paprika

½ teaspoon garlic powder

Dill pickles slices, for serving

French bread, for serving

Preheat the oil in a deep fryer or a cast iron skillet to 360 degrees.

In a medium bowl, whisk the milk, eggs, and hot sauce until combined. In another medium bowl, whisk together the flour, cornstarch, Creole seasoning, and salt.

Rinse the crabs and then pat dry. Dredge the crabs in the flour mixture, then in the milk mixture, then in the flour once more. Be sure to shake off the excess after each step.

Fry the crabs, 2 at a time, until golden brown, 2–3 minutes on each side. Remove from the fryer and place on a wire rack over a baking sheet.

To make the hot coating, melt the butter in a heatproof bowl. Add Worcestershire sauce, cayenne pepper, brown sugar, paprika, and garlic powder. Whisk together until well combined.

Baste the hot coating over each side of the crabs. Serve immediately with pickles and French bread.

SMOTHERED PORK CHOPS AND WILD RICE PLATE LUNCH

MAKES 4 SERVINGS

4 thick-cut bone-in pork chops

3 to 4 tablespoons Creole seasoning

Kosher salt, to taste

1 cup all-purpose flour

2 teaspoons garlic powder

¼ teaspoon chili powder

¼ cup vegetable oil, plus 3 tablespoons
  more, divided

2 sweet onions, thinly sliced

2 tablespoons butter

1½ cups chicken stock

¼ cup heavy cream

Chopped fresh parsley, for garnish

Wild Rice (page 40)

Season pork chops all over with Creole seasoning and salt. In a shallow dish, mix together flour with garlic powder and chili powder. Coat pork chops in flour, shaking off excess. Reserve 2 tablespoons seasoned flour.

In a large, heavy skillet over medium heat, heat ¼ cup oil until shimmering. In batches, cook pork chops until golden, 4-5 minutes per side. Transfer to a plate.

Reduce heat to medium low, pour in remaining oil, add onions, and cook until very soft and slightly caramelized, 15-20 minutes. Add butter and let melt, then sprinkle in reserved seasoned flour. Cook until flour is no longer raw, about 1 minute. Stir in stock and cream and bring to a simmer. Stir until sauce begins to thicken, about 5 minutes.

Return pork chops to skillet and cook until pork is cooked through, about 10 minutes more. Taste and adjust with salt to taste. Garnish with parsley and serve with Wild Rice.

Continued

Wild Rice

MAKES 8 TO 10 SERVINGS

2 cups uncooked wild rice blend

8 cups chicken stock

¼ cup butter, sliced

1 onion, chopped

1 cup baby carrots, thinly sliced

2 cups Brussels sprouts, shaved

4 cloves garlic, minced

1 teaspoon Italian seasoning

¼ teaspoon ground black pepper

Kosher salt

Add wild rice and stock to a large saucepan and bring to a boil over high heat. Lower heat to low and cover. Let rice simmer for 45 minutes, stirring halfway through. When rice is done cooking, strain any remaining liquid from the rice.

While the rice is cooking, add butter to a large, deep skillet over medium-high heat. Once butter is melted and starting to bubble, add onion and carrots. Stir to combine. Cover and cook 5 minutes, stirring occasionally. Add Brussels sprouts, garlic, Italian seasoning, and black pepper, stirring another 2 minutes until softened.

Fluff wild rice with a fork and add to skillet with vegetable mixture, stirring to incorporate. Taste and season with salt as needed.

Note: Vegetable alternatives include chopped bell peppers, broccoli florets, cut green beans, and mushrooms.

COUCHE COUCHE

MAKES 4 SERVINGS

2 cups yellow cornmeal

1 teaspoon kosher salt

1 teaspoon baking powder

1 cup water

2 tablespoons vegetable oil

Milk

Maple or cane syrup

Mix cornmeal, salt, baking powder, and water, being sure that the mixture is not too dry. Add more water if necessary.

Heat oil in a medium skillet and add cornmeal mixture into hot oil. Let the mixture form a crust at the bottom of the skillet.

Stir well and then lower the heat to simmer. Cover and cook about 20 minutes, stirring frequently. Serve with milk and/or maple or cane syrup.

ACADIA PARISH
Rice Central

There are several crops grown in Louisiana that thrive due to our wet, humid climate. Rice is at the top of the list. No one is sure how rice came to South Louisiana, but it definitely made its home here. Medium- and long-grain rice are the most preferred types, and many cooks in Cajun country favor the medium grain. Its shorter grain cooks up soft and a bit sticky, and this is perfect for absorbing sauces and gravies. Almost every meal around here has rice in it in some form, from a scoop of jambalaya, to a fluffy pile with something served over it, to an embellished side dish, to heaping spoonfuls of rice pudding for dessert.

The town of Crowley has become home to the International Rice Festival, which is one of Louisiana's oldest and largest agricultural festivals. To give you an idea of how much rice was being cooked in Cajun country, businessmen with the Japanese company Hitachi visited Southwest Louisiana in the early 1960s because they were curious about the high number of sales of their rice cookers across the region. Upon seeing the miles of rice land and farming operations, they understood. Today, the rice fields serve as a home for more than rice. After harvesting, the fields are stocked with crawfish. So when you are in the area in mid-October and visit the International Rice Festival, as you enjoy that bowl of crawfish étouffée, remember they were both grown in the same field.

BREAKFAST PAELLA

Makes 6 to 8 servings

6 cups chicken stock

1½ teaspoons smoked paprika

Pinch of saffron

Pinch of cayenne pepper

1 pound thick-cut bacon, cut into 1-inch pieces

1 pound smoked sausage, cubed

Extra virgin olive oil

1 onion, diced

1 tablespoon Creole seasoning

½ teaspoon kosher salt

1 (15-ounce) can white beans, drained

1 (14.5-ounce) can crushed tomatoes

2 cups uncooked short- to medium-grain rice

¼ cup chopped flat-leaf parsley

6 hard-boiled eggs, halved

1 roasted red bell pepper, sliced

Lemon wedges

Add the stock, paprika, saffron, and cayenne to a saucepan and set over medium-low heat. When it comes to the simmer, reduce to low and let rest while you assemble the paella.

In a cold 16-inch paella pan or skillet, put the bacon pieces in a single layer. Set the heat to medium-low and gently cook the bacon to start to render the fat. The bacon should not brown or crisp. Once the fat is rendering out, add in the sausage and cook the mixture until both are hot and just starting to color around the edges. Move the bacon and sausage to the sides of the pan, revealing an empty center. Add about 1 tablespoon oil to the bacon fat in the center and add the onion, stirring to cook until just tender, but not browned. Add Creole seasoning, salt, and beans, mix with the onion, and cook for about 1 minute. Combine the meat mixture with the onion mixture then push it all to the sides of the pan again.

Preheat oven to 425 degrees.

If pan is dry, add another half tablespoon of oil and then pour the tomatoes into the center. Cook for 5-7 minutes, stirring regularly, until the tomatoes darken and thicken. Combine the tomatoes with the rest of the ingredients in the pan. Sprinkle the rice evenly over the top and then stir the rice in with the rest of the ingredients. Carefully pour 4 cups of the stock mixture evenly over the rice mixture and bring it to a simmer. Move the pan around periodically to ensure it is boiling evenly. Cook for 7-9 minutes until the liquid is almost even with the rice mixture. If the liquid is being absorbed quickly, spoon some of the reserved stock over the top.

Move the pan to your oven and cook for about 15 minutes. Check the pan about halfway through to see if the rice seems too crunchy; spoon over more stock if needed. Rotate the pan to ensure even cooking. After 15 minutes, check a small spoonful of rice to make sure it is cooked and only a little bit al dente. If it needs more time, check again in 3 minutes.

Remove from the oven, cover with aluminum foil, and let rest for 15 minutes. Remove the foil, sprinkle parsley all over the top, then arrange the hard-boiled egg halves around the edge. Decorate with roasted red pepper slices and serve right in the pan with lemon wedges.

CAJUN SHRIMP BOWL

4 tablespoons melted butter, divided

3 cloves garlic, minced

2 tablespoons Creole seasoning

1⅓ cups uncooked long-grain rice

2⅔ cups chicken stock

½ teaspoon kosher salt

½ cup sliced green onions

1 pound large shrimp, peeled and deveined

Chopped parsley, for garnish

Add 2 tablespoons butter to a large skillet over medium heat. Stir in garlic, Creole seasoning, and rice.

Stir in stock, bring to a boil, reduce to a simmer, and cover. Cook for 15 minutes, stirring 1-2 times throughout.

While rice is cooking, prepare the shrimp by stirring together remaining butter, salt, and green onions. Pour over shrimp and toss to coat.

Stir shrimp into the rice, cover, and cook 3-5 minutes longer until shrimp turns pink and opaque. Garnish with chopped parsley and serve.

CHOCOLATE BUTTERMILK PIE

MAKES 8 SERVINGS

25 Oreo cookies

¾ cup butter, plus 5 tablespoons more, divided

⅓ cup cocoa powder

1½ cups sugar

4 large eggs

2 tablespoons all-purpose flour

1 cup buttermilk

1 tablespoon vanilla extract

¼ teaspoon kosher salt

Preheat oven to 350 degrees.

To make the crust, finely crush the whole Oreo cookies, including the filling. Melt 5 tablespoons of the butter. Stir together the cookie crumbs and the melted butter with a fork. Press this mixture into the bottom and up the sides of a 9-inch pie plate. Bake for 8 minutes, then remove the crust from the oven and allow to cool slightly.

Melt the remaining butter in a medium saucepan over low heat. Add the cocoa powder and sugar, stirring constantly until well blended. Set aside.

In a large bowl, whisk the eggs until light and frothy. Add the flour and buttermilk and continue to whisk until well combined. Slowly add the chocolate mixture, continuing to stir the entire time. Whisk mixture very well or the pie will separate while baking. Add in the vanilla and salt, stirring to incorporate.

Pour the filling into the Oreo crust. Bake for 45 minutes. The edges of the pie will be slightly crusty and the center will still jiggle slightly. Remove to a wire rack and cool. Pie can be served warm or at room temperature.

ST. LANDRY PARISH
Prairie Sampler

The heart of St. Landry Parish is Opelousas, which has given us such great people as Tony Chachere and Chef Paul Prudhomme.

The United States learned about Louisiana seasoning through Tony Chachere (pronounced sas-cher-ree). He was a business man who started his own pharmaceutical wholesale company before switching to the insurance industry. In the early 1970s, his love of Louisiana cuisine called him to create a seasoning that soon found its way into the pantries of people all over the country. Today, Mr. Tony's grandson keeps the business going strong.

Chef Paul took it to the next level and introduced Louisiana flavor to the world. I remember Chef telling me that he learned cooking from the women in his family. I guess in a household of thirteen kids, there is a lot of cooking happening. His sister, Enola, had a restaurant just south of Opelousas that I was fortunate enough to visit for good food, and a chat with her. Chef Paul loved playing with herbs and spices from around the world to take flavors of other cuisines and create dishes using Louisiana ingredients. Probably the most well-known technique Chef created was blackening. This is cooking a piece of fish or meat in a super-heated cast iron pan to create a wonderful sear. That doesn't mean coating the protein with black pepper or burning it. Done right, it is moist and juicy with a crisped exterior.

After Hurricane Katrina, I was staying in Lafayette, and came back to New Orleans for the day. I had heard that K-Paul's, Chef Paul's restaurant, was open, and I was told I should go see him. In true New Orleans' and Chef Paul's style, I got there and he said, "Good, you're here," like he was expecting me. He had a handkerchief in hand, motioned for the musicians follow, and we second-lined through the restaurant. When we were done, he asked me where I was staying, and I told him that I was looking for a place in New Orleans. He said, "Good because you need to be here." He said there was a place he used to own, he knew the owner, and that I needed to call about it. I said I would, I drove by to get the information, and I called the next day. When I called and introduced myself, the owner said, "Kevin?" I said, "Yes sir," and he said, "Chef Paul called me last night and the place is yours as soon as you want it." Not only was Chef Paul just around the corner, but the world-famous artist George Rodrigue was my next-door neighbor. That was Chef Paul. He was an incredible chef, but more importantly, he was an extraordinary man who always looked out for those around him. He will forever be missed.

MY CAJUN KEVIN PO'BOY

MAKES 4 SERVINGS

5 strips thick-cut bacon, diced

2 links andouille sausage, cubed

1 onion, thinly sliced

1 red bell pepper, thinly sliced

1 yellow bell pepper, thinly sliced

5 green onions, sliced

2 tablespoons Creole seasoning

5 cloves garlic, minced

½ pound shrimp

½ pound crawfish tails

¾ cup heavy cream

¼ cup garlic sauce

1 cup grated Parmesan cheese

½ pound crabmeat

Parsley and green onions for garnish

French bread

In a Dutch oven or large cast iron skillet, cook bacon over medium-high heat until crisp. Remove bacon and set aside.

Add andouille, onion, bell peppers, green onions, and Creole seasoning; sauté until onion and peppers are tender, about 5 minutes. Add garlic, stirring for 1 minute to release its flavor. Stir in shrimp and crawfish, cooking for 2 minutes. Add cream and garlic sauce, mixing well and bring to a simmer for 2 minutes. Stir in cheese, crabmeat, and bacon, mixing thoroughly. Remove from heat and garnish with parsley and green onions.

Cut bread into pieces that are 5–6 inches long, trimming the ends. Hollow the bread out leaving a sturdy wall. Stand bread up on plate and spoon the seafood mixture into the bread. You can also use the end pieces to sop up overflowing goodness.

TASSO POTATO CROQUETTES

MAKES 20 CROQUETTES

3 medium potatoes, peeled

3 cloves garlic

½ pound tasso, cubed small

3 large eggs, divided

½ cup grated Romano cheese

1 tablespoon Creole seasoning

1 teaspoon kosher salt

¼ cup chopped parsley

½ cup all-purpose flour

1 cup seasoned breadcrumbs

3 tablespoons olive oil

Parsley, for garnish

Boil potatoes and garlic in a pot filled with water and drain when cooked. Rice or mash potatoes along with the garlic in a large bowl. Add tasso, 1 egg, cheese, Creole seasoning, salt, and parsley, stirring to mix well. Using an ice cream scoop, form 10 balls. Cut each ball in half and shape into a log that is 2-3 inches long. Place croquettes in refrigerator for 15 minutes.

Preheat oven to 375 degrees. Prepare a large baking dish with nonstick cooking spray.

Prepare 3 shallow bowls, 1 for each the flour, 2 eggs beaten with 2 tablespoons water, and the breadcrumbs. Roll each croquette in flour, shaking off excess, in egg, and then in breadcrumbs. In a nonstick skillet over medium heat, add olive oil. Place 5 croquettes in skillet, turning so all sides get coated with oil. Pan fry just until evenly tanned, and place in baking dish. Once all of the croquettes are in the baking dish, bake for 15 minutes. Serve immediately and garnish with parsley.

ZYDECO OMELETTE

Makes 1 to 2 servings

2 slices bacon, diced small

½ link andouille sausage, diced small

1 green onion, sliced thin on the bias

¼ cup diced small red bell pepper

4 large eggs

1 tablespoon butter

½ cup grated Monterey Jack cheese

Pinch of kosher salt

Cook the bacon and sausage, stirring in a medium nonstick skillet over medium heat. Using a slotted spoon, transfer the bacon and sausage to a bowl, leaving the rendered fat in the skillet. Add the onion and bell pepper to the skillet and cook, stirring until softened, 2–3 minutes. Transfer to the bowl with the bacon and sausage. Wipe out the skillet.

In a medium bowl, whisk the eggs. Melt the butter in the cleaned skillet over medium heat. Swirl the pan to coat with the melted butter then pour in eggs. With a rubber spatula or wooden spoon, starting from the outer edge, scrape the egg toward the middle of the pan to remove cooked egg from the bottom and make way for raw egg to cook. Do this several times until the raw egg is mostly cooked and you have a thin layer of raw egg on top. Lower the heat, if needed, to maintain the pale yellow of the egg and avoid browning.

To flip the omelette, loosen the egg from the skillet by running the spatula around the edges and jiggling the pan. In one motion, front to back, slide the eggs forward so that they flop over and move the pan back under the eggs. If you are not familiar with this technique, you can practice it with a piece of bread in the same clean pan. The key is to move the pan up and down as little as possible.

Working quickly to avoid browning the eggs, top the flipped omelette with the cheese, bacon, sausage, onion, bell pepper, and salt. Run the spatula around the edge of the omelette again to loosen. Slide the omelette halfway out of the pan onto the plate and tilt the pan to fold the omelette onto itself. Serve immediately.

EVANGELINE PARISH

Cajun Heartland

I first met Mr. Ortego in 1992, while he was on a weekend trip to New Orleans. At this point, I had been using his hot sauce for years in my cooking, as well as it having a place on my table for additional seasoning. Something about this sauce was different from others, and I couldn't put my finger on it. It wasn't until years later that I found out what made his sauce special. During a sit down with Mr. Ortego, he told me he grew the peppers, picked them, graded them, and made the sauce himself. The other thing he said that was so important, was the fact that all the peppers grew in Louisiana soil in Evangeline Parish. After being in the military and returning home, he started different businesses, but always had a passion for food. He played with the recipe over many years until he was happy with his sauce. I loved how he would keep some in the trunk of his car early on, and when asked about the sauce, he would give you a bottle to try.

Mr. Ortega started his sauce business in the small town of Ville Platte, located on the edge of the Cajun prairie. The northern portion of Evangeline Parish is where we start to have some rolling hills, but don't get too excited, they're only slightly rolling. They say that good things come in small packages. Ortego Hot Sauce came in a small bottle, was made in a small town, by a man with a huge heart. It was an honor and a pleasure to call Mr. Ortego a friend. The sauce is no longer made since Mr. Ortego has passed away.

SAUSAGE AND PORK JAMBALAYA

MAKES 6 TO 8 SERVINGS

5 strips thick-cut bacon, diced

1 pound pork loin or butt, cubed

½ pound andouille sausage, cut half rounds

½ pound smoked sausage, sliced

½ cup cubed tasso

2 cups diced onion

1 cup diced celery

1 cup diced bell pepper (your choice of color)

4 cloves garlic, minced

2 tablespoons Creole seasoning

1 teaspoon kosher salt

2½ cups beef stock

3 tablespoons Kitchen Bouquet

2 cups uncooked long-grain rice

Parsley and green onion, for garnish

In a large Dutch oven, cook bacon over medium-high heat until crisp; remove and set aside. Add pork, andouille, smoked sausage, and tasso. Sauté the meats for 5 minutes, stirring periodically, allowing meat to brown. Add onion, celery, bell pepper, garlic, Creole seasoning, and salt. Mix well, and cook for 3-5 minutes.

Pour in stock and Kitchen Bouquet and bring to a boil. Add rice, stir well, and bring back to a boil. Reduce heat and simmer for 10 minutes. Turn off heat, stir in parsley and green onion, and allow to rest, covered, for 15 minutes.

HOT SAUCE WITH FERMENTED PEPPERS

MAKES 1 ¼ CUPS SAUCE

1 pound red serrano or jalapeño peppers

4 cups distilled water

3 tablespoons kosher salt

½ to 1 cup white or red wine vinegar

Roughly chop the peppers and place them into a wide-mouth quart-size Mason jar, packing them tight and leaving 1 inch from the top of the jar. The peppers will rise when fermenting.

Mix the water with the salt. Pour enough brine over the peppers to cover, pressing down the peppers as you go. Close the jar with the lid and store in a cool spot, ideally 55–75 degrees. Never store the jar in direct sunlight. Check the jar daily to make sure the peppers are covered with the brine. The active fermentation takes place between 1–2 weeks. During this time, gases will accumulate, so everyday unscrew the lid to allow the gas to escape then retighten.

After 1–2 weeks, the fermenting will diminish and the brine will be cloudy. Drain the peppers, reserving the brine. Add the peppers to a food processor or blender with ½ cup of the brine and ½ cup vinegar. Adding more brine will have more of a salty flavor, while more vinegar will be more acidic. Process until smooth. Pour the sauce into a pot and bring to a boil on high heat. Once boiling, reduce heat to low, and simmer for 15 minutes. Strain the mixture to remove solids if desired, or use as is for a thicker sauce. You can add more vinegar or water to thin if desired. Pour into bottles and enjoy.

CRACKLIN' CORNBREAD

MAKES 8 TO 10 SERVINGS

1 cup butter, divided

2 cups self-rising cornmeal

½ cup all-purpose flour

2 tablespoons sugar

½ teaspoon kosher salt

2½ cups buttermilk

2 eggs, beaten

1 cup cracklins

Preheat oven to 425 degrees.

Place ¼ cup butter in a 9-inch cast iron skillet and put into oven until butter is melted; remove from oven.

Combine cornmeal, flour, sugar, and salt in a large bowl, making a well in the middle. Stir together buttermilk, eggs, and cracklins. Add to the dry ingredients, stirring just enough to combine. Melt the remaining butter and add to the mixture. Pour the batter into the hot skillet with the melted butter. Bake for 25–30 minutes until golden brown and an inserted toothpick comes out clean.

Note: You can use 12 to 15 slices of bacon, cut in small pieces and cooked, as a substitute for cracklin.

RAPIDES PARISH
Heart of Louisiana

My wife Monica is not from Louisiana. She came here, bringing Noah, who was eight years old at the time, to be with me. I have made it my mission to show them all the great things that Louisiana has to offer. We just head out in different directions to see all the sights.

On one particular day, we drove out to Alexandria in Rapides Parish, which is about a three-hour ride from New Orleans, and decided to visit the Alexandria Zoological Park. We had a wonderful visit to the zoo, and something happened that I will never forget. Monica and Noah were a step or two ahead of me and Monica reached out for Noah's hand, as moms often do. And then Noah looked back and reached out for my hand. That very moment choked me up and I may have even shed a tear. From that time on, I knew that little boy was mine, and I love him as if he were my own. That by far was the best day Alexandria could offer us as a family.

PAN-FRIED BASS WITH LEMON-GARLIC HERB SAUCE

MAKES 4 SERVINGS

1½ pounds bass fillets

1 to 2 tablespoons Creole seasoning

¼ cup all-purpose flour

1 teaspoon kosher salt, plus more if needed

½ teaspoon black pepper, plus more if needed

3 tablespoons butter, divided

1 tablespoon olive oil

¼ cup dry white wine

2 cloves garlic, minced

1 tablespoon chopped fresh oregano

1 tablespoon chopped fresh thyme

1 tablespoon chopped fresh parsley

½ cup chicken stock

1 lemon, juiced

Lemon wedges, for serving

Pat the fish dry with a paper towel and sprinkle Creole seasoning on both sides.

In a shallow dish, mix together the flour, salt, and pepper. Dredge each piece of fish in the flour mixture, coating the entire surface, and shake off any excess.

In a large skillet, preferably nonstick, melt 1 tablespoon of the butter over medium-high heat and add the oil.

Cook the fish in the skillet for 3–4 minutes on each side, until golden brown and fully cooked. Do not move the fish too much, especially if you are using a pan that isn't nonstick, otherwise the fish may stick to the bottom and not get browned as nicely as it should. Remove fish from the skillet to a plate.

Turn down the heat to low. Add the white wine to the skillet to deglaze, stirring up any browned bits. Continue heating until almost all the wine has evaporated.

Add 1 more tablespoon of butter to the skillet. Once it's melted, add the garlic and fresh herbs to the skillet and sauté until fragrant, about 30 seconds. Add the stock and bring to a simmer. Turn off heat and stir in remaining butter and lemon juice. Taste and adjust seasoning if necessary. Serve sauce on top of fish.

BISCUITS AND SAUSAGE GRAVY

Makes 4 to 6 servings

Biscuits

6 tablespoons cold butter

2 cups all-purpose flour

1 tablespoon baking powder

1 tablespoon sugar

1 teaspoon kosher salt

¾ cup cold milk

Sausage Gravy

1 pound pork breakfast sausage

¼ cup all-purpose flour

2½ cups milk

1 teaspoon Creole seasoning

½ teaspoon kosher salt

⅛ teaspoon crushed red pepper, optional

Biscuits

Chill butter in the freezer for 10-20 minutes before beginning this recipe. The very cold butter makes light, flaky, buttery biscuits.

Preheat oven to 425 degrees and line a baking sheet with parchment paper.

Combine flour, baking powder, sugar, and salt in a large bowl and mix well. Remove butter from the freezer and cut it into the flour mixture using a pastry cutter until the mixture resembles coarse crumbs. Add the milk to the flour mixture and stir until just combined, don't overmix.

Transfer the biscuit dough to a clean, well-floured surface, and use your hands to gently work the dough together. If the dough is too sticky, add flour until it is manageable.

Once the dough is cohesive, fold in half over itself and use your hands to gently flatten. Rotate the dough 90 degrees and fold in half again, repeat this step 5-6 times, taking care to not overwork the dough. Use your hands to gently flatten the dough to 1 inch thick.

Press a 2¾-inch-wide biscuit cutter straight down into the dough and drop the biscuit onto the prepared baking sheet. Repeat until you have gotten as many biscuits as possible, and place them less than ½ inch apart on baking sheet.

Once you have cut as many biscuits as possible out of the dough, gently rework the dough to cut out another biscuit or two until you have at least 7 biscuits total. Bake for 10-12 minutes or until tops are lightly golden brown.

Prepare gravy while the biscuits are baking.

Sausage Gravy

Place sausage in a skillet and turn heat to medium high. Cook, crumbling the sausage as it cooks, until no pink remains. Do not drain the skillet.

Sprinkle the flour evenly over the sausage crumbles and cook a minute longer until the flour is absorbed. Slowly pour the milk into skillet, stirring as you pour. Add Creole seasoning, salt, and crushed red pepper, if using. Cook, stirring, until mixture is thickened.

Once biscuits are finished baking, slice in half, and ladle gravy over biscuits.

KOLACHES

MAKES 12 SMALL KOLACHES

Fillings

6 prunes

1 tablespoon honey

Water

4 scoops apricot preserves

3 ounces cream cheese, room temperature

1 tablespoon powdered sugar

Dough

2/3 cup milk

2 teaspoons active dry yeast

3 tablespoons sugar

6 tablespoons butter, melted

1 large egg

2 cups all-purpose flour

1/2 teaspoon kosher salt

1 egg, beaten

Splash of heavy cream or milk

Make the 3 different fillings. If you want all of the kolaches to be the same, triple 1 of the filling recipes.

Prune Filling

Combine the prunes in a small saucepan with the honey, and add enough water to come halfway on the prunes. Bring to a boil, stirring occasionally, for about 10 minutes. Mash the prunes with a fork as they cook. They're done when most of the water is evaporated and it's thicker than jam. Set aside to cool.

Apricot Filling

Have the apricot preserves ready in a small bowl.

Cream Cheese Filling

Stir together the cream cheese with the powdered sugar until smooth. Set aside.

Dough

Warm the milk to 110 degrees. Once at 110 degrees, pour it into a large bowl and add the yeast and sugar. Allow yeast to foam and bloom.

In another bowl, add the melted butter. Let cool briefly before stirring in egg. Add this to the yeast mixture and mix well. Mix flour and salt together. Add 1/2 cup of flour mixture at a time to yeast mixture and mix well after each addition.

Sprinkle flour on a board and your hands and knead the dough for 10 minutes. At the end of 10 minutes, the dough will be soft, supple, and not sticky at all. Spray a bowl with nonstick cooking spray

and add the dough. Cover and let rise in a warm place until it doubles in size, about an hour.

Divide the dough into 12 equal portions. Roll each dough ball into a perfect circle. Line a 9 x 13-inch baking sheet with parchment paper and arrange the dough balls on it. Spray a towel or plastic wrap with nonstick cooking spray and cover the balls. Set in a warm place and let dough rise until balls are nearly double in size, 30–60 minutes.

Preheat oven to 375 degrees.

Once the dough balls are double in size, use your fingers to make indentations for the fillings. Stir together the egg and heavy cream to use as the egg wash for the rolls.

Divide the fillings between the kolaches, and then brush with the egg wash, trying not to get egg wash on the fillings.

Bake the kolaches for 18–20 minutes, until golden brown. Use a toothpick inserted into the center kolache to ensure the rolls are done. Let cool slightly and serve.

AVOYELLES PARISH
Smack Dab in the Middle

Avoyelles is known for its French Colonial History, and the use of the French language by many people living in the parish. Native Americans have lived here on the banks of the Mississippi River for centuries, and the contemporary Creole traditions reflect European, African, and Native American influences.

I remember my first trip to Avoyelles Parish. I was traveling with the Association France-Louisiane, and we visited the town of Mansura for an event. The evening dinner was hosted on a family farm where the main attraction was a pig laying between rebar mesh hanging and spinning slowly over an open fire. It was a celebration of food where the culmination was the pig being done. The glorious 100-pound pig was taken down, cut up in pieces, and shredded to accompany all the sides of veggies, grains, casseroles, and breads.

Every May Mansura is the home to the Cochon de Lait Festival, which is a Cajun pig roast. I have made many trips since that first visit to this wonderful town to see the sight of countless pigs slowly turning as they transform into crispy deliciousness. Of course, there is music, food, and competition, from hog calling, to boudin eating, to chasing greased pigs, which if you catch one, you get to keep it. This is where family, friends, food, and fun come together to make harmony.

SMOKED MEAT GUMBO

MAKES 8 TO 12 SERVINGS

3 tablespoons vegetable oil, plus 1 cup more, divided

1 pound andouille sausage, sliced into half moons

½ pound smoked sausage, sliced

¼ pound tasso, cubed small

1 to 2 smoked ham hocks

½ pound smoked turkey, cubed

2 cups chopped onions

1 cup chopped celery

1 cup chopped green bell pepper

1 cup all-purpose flour

2 cloves garlic, minced

3 bay leaves

1 tablespoon kosher salt

2 tablespoons Creole seasoning

8 to 10 cups chicken stock

Parsley and green onions, chopped, for garnish

Cooked rice, for serving

In a stockpot, heat 3 tablespoons oil over medium heat. Add andouille, smoked sausage, tasso, ham hocks, and turkey and sauté for 3-5 minutes. Remove from heat and add onions, celery, and bell pepper; set aside.

In a stainless steel or cast iron pan, heat 1 cup oil over medium-high heat. Add flour, and use a whisk to slowly stir, making sure to cover the entire bottom of the pan until flour is a chocolate color. Pour roux on top of vegetables in stockpot and stir. Place pot over medium heat, add garlic, bay leaves, salt, and Creole seasoning, and stir for 2 minutes. Add stock and bring to a boil. Reduce heat and simmer for 45 minutes to 1 hour. Stir in parsley, and green onions. Serve over cooked rice.

Note: Once the gumbo boils, it can simmer for hours. The longer it cooks, the more the flavors blend. Keep in mind if you are adding shrimp, they only need to cook for the last 10 minutes before serving.

CRISPY GLAZED DUCK ON STONE-GROUND GRITS

Makes 4 servings

Duck

¼ cup hoisin sauce

¼ cup rice wine

½ teaspoon five-spice powder

1 inch ginger, sliced

4 cloves garlic, coarsely chopped

4 duck breasts

½ teaspoon kosher salt

Grits

2 cups chicken stock

3 cups milk

1 teaspoon kosher salt

1 cup stone-ground grits

4 tablespoons butter

1 to 2 cups grated Gruyère

Parsley and green onions, for garnish

Duck

Combine hoisin, rice wine, five-spice powder, ginger, and garlic in a food processor or blender and pulse until it forms a runny paste. Pour into a 12-inch baking dish.

Pat duck dry with paper towels then place in the dish with the marinade, skin side up. Sprinkle salt on the skin. Marinate, uncovered, in the refrigerator for a couple hours to overnight. Take the duck out of the fridge at least 20 minutes before cooking, so it will return to room temperature.

Preheat oven to 425 degrees.

Before cooking, pat the duck dry with paper towels. Score the skin in a ½-inch diamond pattern.

Over medium heat in a 12-inch heavy skillet, place duck skin side down. Cook until the skin turns golden brown, about 6–8 minutes. Flip duck and cook for 3–4 minutes. Once cooked, flip so duck is skin side down once again.

Transfer the skillet to the oven and bake for 8 minutes. Flip the duck to skin side up and bake for another 6–8 minutes, until the skin turns dark brown. Transfer the duck to a big plate, skin side up. Allow to rest for 10 minutes without cover before carving.

Grits

Add stock, milk, and salt to a heavy saucepan and bring to a boil. Gradually whisk in the grits, a little at a time, stirring continuously to prevent any lumps. Reduce heat to barely a simmer and cook grits, covered but stirring frequently, until stock is fully absorbed and grits are thickened, about 15 minutes. Remove grits from heat. Add butter and cheese, stirring with a whisk until cheese melts. Adjust salt if needed.

To assemble the dish, place grits at the bottom of individual plates and top with duck. Garnish with parsley and green onions.

CREOLE-SPICED MIXED NUTS

MAKES 12 SERVINGS

2 tablespoons bacon grease

2 cloves garlic, minced

2 cups peanuts (salted or unsalted)

1 cup cashews (salted or unsalted)

1 cup whole almonds

1 cup pecan halves

½ tablespoon Creole seasoning

½ teaspoon kosher salt

2 teaspoons sugar

1 teaspoon pepper

Preheat oven to 200 degrees.

In a small saucepan, heat bacon grease over low heat. Add garlic and cook for 2-3 minutes.

Place nuts in a large bowl. Drizzle bacon fat and garlic over nuts and toss to coat. Sprinkle Creole seasoning, salt, sugar, and pepper over nuts. Toss to coat evenly.

Pour nuts onto a large baking sheet and place in oven for 45 minutes, stirring every 15 minutes. Allow to cool before serving.

Creole Seasoning

MAKES ABOUT ⅓ CUP SEASONING

¼ cup kosher salt

1 tablespoon onion powder

2 tablespoons paprika

½ tablespoon cayenne pepper

1 tablespoon garlic powder

1 teaspoon white pepper

1 teaspoon black pepper

½ teaspoon dry mustard

½ teaspoon dried oregano

½ teaspoon dried thyme

In a small bowl, combine all ingredients. Store in a small jar with a lid.

TOLEDO BEND
Lake Country

When I hear the words Toledo Bend, I immediately envision myself looking out over a beautiful lake with a fishing pole in one hand and a tackle box in the other. I can comfortably say that most Louisianans are drawn to water, and this area in Sabine Parish is one of the best. We are talking about an area of 185,000 acres of water, the largest man-made body of water in Louisiana. It is actually a reservoir, but people refer to it as a lake. We do share part of it with Texas because it sits on Louisiana's western border, and it is near Fort Polk Army Base. You can swim, boat, picnic, fish, camp, sightsee, hike, and just relax with a book. It's definitely a place to go to get away and recharge your battery from the everyday routine. I really need to go there more often.

ZWOLLE HOT TAMALES

4½ cups chicken stock, divided

2 cups corn kernels

3¾ cups masa harina

1½ teaspoons salt

1½ teaspoons baking powder

½ cup lard, plus 2 tablespoons more, chilled, divided

60 dried corn husks

1 onion, chopped

1 tablespoon Creole seasoning

5 cloves garlic, crushed

2 pounds pulled pork, chopped

Combine 2½ cups stock and corn in a blender; process until smooth. Set aside.

In a bowl, combine masa harina, salt, and baking powder; stir well with a whisk. Cut in ½ cup lard with a pastry blender until mixture resembles coarse meal. Add stock and corn purée; stir until a soft dough forms. Cover and chill at least 1 hour but preferably overnight.

Place corn husks in a large bowl; cover with water. Weigh husks down with a weight and soak for at least 30 minutes.

Melt remaining lard in a skillet over medium-high heat. Add onion and sauté until browned, about 10 minutes. Add Creole seasoning and garlic and sauté for 2 minutes. Add remaining stock and bring to a boil. Reduce heat to medium-low and simmer until liquid is reduced to ½ cup. Add pulled pork and combine well. Taste and adjust seasoning.

Place about 3 tablespoons masa dough on center of a husk, pressing into a rectangle and leaving at least ½ inch of room on all sides. Spoon 1 heaping tablespoon pork mixture on top of dough. Fold husk over filling, covering the meat with dough; fold husk over once more before folding bottom end of husk underneath. Repeat the process with the remaining husks, dough, and pork. Evenly place tamales in a steamer basket positioned in a large pot filled with water. Bring the water to a boil, reduce heat, and steam 1 hour. If all of the tamales don't fit into your steamer basket, you may need to steam in batches.

LOUISIANA FISH ON THE HALF SHELL

MAKES 4 SERVINGS

6 tablespoons butter, softened

1 tablespoon finely chopped shallot

1 tablespoon chopped cilantro

1 teaspoon chopped thyme

½ teaspoon garlic powder

½ teaspoon paprika

1 teaspoon kosher salt, or to taste

4 boneless redfish, snapper, or sheepshead
   fillets with scales left on

1 tablespoon vegetable oil

2 tablespoons Creole seasoning

12 thin lemon rounds

Heat a large cast iron skillet over medium-high heat.

Put butter, shallot, cilantro, thyme, garlic powder, paprika, and salt into a bowl. Using a hand mixer, whip mixture until fluffy. Brush scales of fish with oil. Flip fillets, season flesh with Creole seasoning, and smear each with 1 tablespoon butter mixture. Top each fillet with 3 lemon rounds.

Place fish, scale side down, in skillet and cover. Cook, basting occasionally with remaining butter mixture, until fish is cooked through, 8–10 minutes.

BLACKBERRY PIE

6 cups blackberries

½ cup sugar

1 teaspoon kosher salt

⅓ cup cornstarch

1 lemon, zested

1 tablespoon lemon juice

½ teaspoon cinnamon

2 pie crusts

1 tablespoon butter

1 large egg

1 tablespoon milk

1 tablespoon coarse sanding sugar

Preheat oven to 375 degrees.

In a large bowl, gently toss the blackberries, sugar, salt, cornstarch, lemon zest and juice, and cinnamon. Let rest while you prepare the crust.

Line 1 (9-inch) pie pan with 1 crust and keep it in the refrigerator while you make a lattice topping with the second crust.

Add the blackberry filling to the pie pan. Cut the butter into thin slices and distribute evenly over the pie filling.

Cover with the lattice crust then fold the edges of the lattice under the back of the bottom layer of pie crust and pinch them together to seal. Mix egg and milk together and brush it onto the pie crust. Sprinkle coarse sanding sugar over the top.

Bake for 30 minutes then reduce oven temperature to 350 degrees and bake an additional 30 minutes. If the pie is browning too quickly, tent it lightly with a piece of aluminum foil to prevent additional browning. Cool pie before slicing so the filling can thicken.

Pie Crust

MAKES 1 (9-INCH) DOUBLE-CRUST PIE OR 2 (9-INCH) SINGLE-CRUST PIES

2½ cups all-purpose flour, divided

1 teaspoon kosher salt

1 tablespoon sugar

1 cup cold butter, cut into ½-inch cubes

4 to 8 tablespoons ice water

Continued

Add 1½ cups flour, salt, and sugar to a food processor. Pulse 2-3 times until combined. Scatter butter cubes over flour and process until a dough begins to form, about 15 seconds.

Scrape bowl, redistribute the mixture, and then add remaining flour. Pulse 4-5 times until flour is evenly distributed. Dough should look broken up and a little crumbly.

Transfer to a medium bowl then sprinkle ice water over mixture. Start with 4 tablespoons and add from there. Using a rubber spatula, press the dough into itself. The crumbs should begin to form larger clusters. If you pinch the dough and it holds together, it's ready. If the dough falls apart, add 2-4 more tablespoons of water and continue to press until dough comes together.

Remove dough from bowl and place in a mound on a clean surface. Work the dough just enough to form a ball. Cut ball in half then form each half into discs. Wrap each disc with plastic wrap and refrigerate at least 1 hour, and up to 2 days.

Remove dough discs from the refrigerator and let sit at room temperature for 5 minutes before rolling out into a crust.

NATICHOCHES
and the Cane River

For an area that sees no snow or freezing temperatures, and is not the official home of the Claus family, Natichoches is Christmas at its best. I had heard for years how Natichoches (pronounced nack-a-tish) celebrates Christmas like no other place in Louisiana. The first time you see it, you are magically transformed into that four-year-old wide-eyed child mesmerized by twinkling lights and the holidays. Understand that we are talking about the oldest European settlement founded by a French explorer in the Louisiana Purchase, which is why to this day,

instead of Santa, people know and refer to him as Papa Noel (or St. Nick). Just think of Papa Noel as the French version of Santa Claus.

Every part of downtown Natichoches is decorated with lights along with magnificent set pieces lining the banks of the Cane River. Of course, there is also food to be had and enjoyed while viewing the sights. I get a couple of meat pies, which are to Natichoches what beignets are to New Orleans. Find a seat along the river, meat pies in hand along with your favorite beverage, and try to catch a glimpse of Papa Noel.

CREOLE POT PIE

4 tablespoons butter

4 tablespoons all-purpose flour

½ cup chopped onion

¼ cup chopped celery

¼ cup chopped green bell pepper

2 cloves garlic, minced

2 cups chicken stock

2 small red-skinned potatoes, diced

2 carrots, diced

1 cup chicken, cooked and shredded

½ pound andouille sausage, diced

1 teaspoon Worcestershire sauce

1 teaspoon hot sauce

1 tablespoon Creole seasoning

1 teaspoon salt

1 tablespoon parsley

1 roll puff pastry, thawed in the refrigerator the night before using

1 large egg beaten with 1 tablespoon water

Preheat oven to 375 degrees.

In a medium pot, melt butter over medium-low heat until a mildly browned. Whisk in flour and continue to cook until the roux is brown.

Add in onion, celery, and bell pepper and cook until tender. Add in garlic and cook for 1 minute.

Whisk in stock, add potatoes, carrots, chicken, and andouille. Simmer on low until stew has thickened and ingredients are tender.

Add in Worcestershire sauce, hot sauce, Creole seasoning, salt, and parsley and lightly stir together. Adjust seasoning to taste. Ladle stew into oven-safe ramekins.

Roll out puff pastry on floured surface. Cut out rounds larger than the size of the ramekins. Brush the sides of the ramekins with egg wash and place puff pastry rounds on top of each ramekin.

Brush the tops of each puff pastry round with egg wash and cut 2 small slits in each pastry. Bake for 30–35 minutes or until puff pastry has puffed and is golden brown and inside filling is bubbly. Remove pot pies from oven to cool for 5–10 minutes before serving.

SLOW-COOKED BBQ
BEEF SANDWICH

MAKES 12 SERVINGS

1 (3-pound) boneless beef chuck roast

1 cup ketchup

¼ cup packed brown sugar

¾ cup barbecue sauce

2 tablespoons Worcestershire sauce

2 tablespoons Dijon mustard

1 teaspoon liquid smoke

1 tablespoon Creole seasoning

½ teaspoon salt

¼ teaspoon garlic powder

¼ teaspoon pepper

12 sandwich buns, buttered and toasted

Sliced onions, dill pickles, and pickled
   jalapeños, optional

Cut roast in half and place in a 3- or 4-quart slow cooker. In a small bowl, combine the ketchup, brown sugar, barbecue sauce, Worcestershire sauce, mustard, liquid smoke, and seasonings. Pour over beef.

Cover and cook on low for 8–10 hours, or until meat is tender. Remove meat and cool slightly. Skim fat from cooking liquid.

Shred beef with 2 forks then return to the slow cooker. Cover and cook for 15 minutes or until heated through. Using a slotted spoon, place ½ cup meat on each bun. Serve with onions, pickles, and jalapeños if desired.

SPICY PECAN BALLS

MAKES 10 TO 12 SERVINGS

2 (8-ounce) packages cream cheese, softened

3 jalapeños, seeded and finely chopped, divided

1 cup grated pepper jack cheese

8 slices bacon, cooked and crumbled, divided

¼ cup chopped green onions

1 tablespoon Creole seasoning

½ teaspoon salt

2 cloves garlic, minced

1 tablespoon Worcestershire sauce

¼ teaspoon cumin

½ cup pecan halves, finely chopped

In a medium bowl, stir together cream cheese, half of the jalapeños, cheese, half of the bacon, green onions, Creole seasoning, salt, garlic, Worcestershire sauce, and cumin until fully incorporated.

On a large plate, combine remaining bacon, remaining jalapeños, and pecans. Shape the cream cheese mixture into a large ball or 10 to 12 individual balls and roll onto the plate to coat well.

Cover with plastic wrap and chill for an hour before serving. Store leftovers in the fridge for up to 3 days.

RED RIVER RICHES
Northwest Louisiana

Shreveport-Bossier City is the largest eco-
nomic and cultural center of North Louisiana.
The area is also called Ark-La-Tex because
this is where the three states come together.
The Red River divides the two cities, but they
seem to always be referred to as Shreveport-
Bossier. Whenever I am in the area, I always
include time to find a quiet spot and watch
the planes take off and land from Barksdale
Air Force Base. If I'm lucky, I get to see a B-52
Stratofortress, which is considered the grandfather of the Air Force. We are talking about a
huge beast of a plane that just looks so graceful
in flight. I guess it's like when I played sports
and people would say, "How can someone your
size move like that?"

As long as I can remember, my dad had a thing
for engines. I watched him work on anything
that had a motor, from a hand mixer to a car
and everything in between. One day, I found
books, medals, maps, and patches and asked
Dad about them. He told me he had been a
member of the Army Air Corps, which would
eventually become the U.S. Air Force. Then he
sat me down and pulled out pictures of airplane
engines, different planes, and photos of himself
and fellow servicemen stationed in Germany. I
thought it funny that someone who had a fear
of heights would be in the Air Corps. Watching
the planes at Barksdale flying overhead make
me smile and remind me of my dad in those pictures. Thanks to all who served then and now.

CHICKEN-FRIED STEAK

4 (6-ounce) top round steaks

2 tablespoons Creole seasoning

1 cup milk or buttermilk

1 large egg

1 cup all-purpose flour

¼ cup cornstarch

1 teaspoon garlic powder

1 teaspoon onion powder

½ teaspoon cayenne pepper

Kosher salt

Freshly ground black pepper

Vegetable oil, for frying

Gravy

4 tablespoons butter

¼ cup all-purpose flour

2 cups milk

½ cup chicken stock

Kosher salt

Freshly ground black pepper

½ teaspoon paprika

¼ cup chopped parsley

Sprinkle steaks with Creole seasoning and place steak between 2 pieces of plastic wrap and pound with a meat mallet until ¼ inch thick.

In a shallow bowl, whisk together milk and egg. In another shallow bowl, whisk together flour, cornstarch, garlic powder, onion powder, and cayenne pepper then season with salt and pepper.

Dredge each piece of steak in milk then in flour mixture. Place in refrigerator while you make gravy.

To make the gravy, melt butter in a large skillet over medium heat. Add flour and cook until golden and bubbling, 2–3 minutes. Whisk in milk and stock and season with salt, pepper, and paprika. Bring mixture to a simmer and cook until slightly thickened, 3–4 minutes. Remove from heat.

In a large skillet over medium heat, heat ½ to 1 inch oil. Fry each steak until golden, about 4 minutes per side. Drain on a paper towel–lined plate, and season with salt and pepper while hot.

Garnish with parsley and serve hot with gravy.

CORNISH GAME HENS WITH CARROT SOUFFLÉ

MAKES 4 SERVINGS

Cornish Game Hens

3 tablespoons olive oil

1 tablespoon Creole seasoning

½ teaspoon kosher salt

¼ teaspoon black pepper

¼ teaspoon crushed rosemary

½ teaspoon lemon zest

¼ teaspoon thyme leaves

2 Cornish game hens

Preheat oven to 425 degrees.

Combine oil, Creole seasoning, salt, pepper, rosemary, lemon zest, and thyme in a small bowl. Brush hens with oil mixture. Twist wings to tuck under the bird.

Place hens in a large casserole dish or on a rimmed baking sheet and put into the oven. Reduce heat to 400 degrees. Bake 55–65 minutes, or just until hens reach 165 degrees with a thermometer.

Remove from the oven and loosely tent with aluminum foil for 10 minutes before cutting. Cut hens in half using kitchen scissors and serve.

Carrot Soufflé

MAKES 8 SERVINGS

3½ pounds carrots, peeled

2½ cups sugar

½ teaspoon salt

1 tablespoon baking powder

1 tablespoon vanilla extract

¼ cup all-purpose flour

6 eggs

½ cup butter, softened

1 tablespoon powdered sugar, for garnish

Preheat oven to 350 degrees.

Steam or boil carrots until extra soft. Drain well. While carrots are warm, add sugar, salt, baking powder, and vanilla. Whip carrots with mixer until smooth. Add flour and mix well.

Whip eggs then add to carrot mixture, blending well. Add butter to the mixture and combine.

Pour mixture into 9 x 13-inch baking dish, filling half full as the soufflé will rise. Bake about 1 hour or until the top is a light golden brown. Sprinkle lightly with powdered sugar over top before serving.

CHESS PIE

1 (9-inch) unbaked pie crust (page 83)

4 large eggs

2 tablespoons cornmeal

1 tablespoon all-purpose flour

1 teaspoon vanilla extract

¼ cup buttermilk

⅓ cup butter, melted

½ teaspoon ground nutmeg

1 tablespoon lemon juice

1½ cups sugar

Preheat oven to 325 degrees.

Place the pie crust in a 9-inch pie pan, line the bottom of pie crust with parchment paper, and add dried beans on top. The beans will ensure that the bottom of the crust does not rise. Bake for 5–6 minutes, remove from the oven, and let cool. Remove the beans and parchment paper.

In a large mixing bowl, combine the eggs, cornmeal, flour, vanilla, buttermilk, butter, nutmeg, lemon juice, and sugar.

Pour the mixture into the pie crust and bake for 35–40 minutes or until the top is thoroughly browned or when a skewer inserted in the middle of the pie comes out clean. Let it cool for 10–12 minutes.

If the pie is a bit runny in the middle, turn off the oven, and leave the pie inside the oven for 5–10 minutes. It's perfectly normal for pie to crack.

If you want to dress up this pie, serve it with berries and whipped cream.

SPORTSMAN'S PARADISE

As a kid, I noticed that on my parents' license plates were the words "Sportsman's Paradise." I really thought about it as I grew. And my thoughts on Louisiana being a sportsman's paradise have definitely grown and expanded. In 1967, the New Orleans Saints played their first football game here in New Orleans. At the time, the city also had a minor league baseball team. They played from 1887–1977. On Fridays, the city was abuzz with everyone talking about their favorite high school football teams as well as the rivalry between Tulane and LSU. It was practically a city holiday when those teams met up in competition. Now we also have the New Orleans Pelicans, our professional basketball team.

As I got older, I completely reassessed my views of the Sportsman's Paradise. It's not just about sports games. My dad and uncle Chet were avid fisherman who loved being outdoors surrounded by all the beauty and nature that Louisiana has to offer. We have so many swamps, bayous, marshes, and lakes where fishing and wildlife are readily available. You can almost drop a line in a puddle and catch anything from bass, sac au lait, speckled trout, redfish, flounder, drum, catfish, and so many more. And for hunters, in the lush, green forest land there is a bounty of squirrels, rabbits, turkey, and deer. From November to January, waterfowl is the focus of hunters for mallards, pintails, red-head ducks, and geese. But there is so much more than just fishing and hunting taking place in our bayous and rivers. Plenty of folks kayak, bird watch, bike the trails, camp, and picnic. There is something for everyone. Living in Louisiana is like living in a pantry. We not only do these activities, but we eat everything we catch, trap, hunt, and grow. What's your adventure of choice?

FRIED QUAIL WITH PEACH CHUTNEY

2 cups buttermilk

2 tablespoons Creole seasoning

2 tablespoons Italian seasoning

2 teaspoons paprika

1 tablespoon garlic powder

1 teaspoon cayenne pepper

8 to 16 quail, depending on size, cut in half

3 cups vegetable oil

1 cup all-purpose flour

1 cup cornstarch

1 tablespoon kosher salt

Combine the buttermilk with the Creole seasoning, Italian seasoning, paprika, garlic powder, and cayenne in a large container. Add the quail and coat with the mixture. Cover and marinate for least 1 hour, or as much as 8 hours.

When you are ready to fry, pour the oil into a large pan and heat over medium-high heat. You want enough oil to almost submerge the quail halves. While the oil is heating, take the quail out of the buttermilk and let drain in a colander. Don't shake off the buttermilk.

When the oil is about 325 degrees, place the flour, cornstarch, and salt into a plastic bag and shake to combine. Put a few quail into the bag and shake to coat the pieces in flour mixture. If you want the quail extra crispy, let the battered birds sit on a rack until the flour absorbs the moisture of the buttermilk coating. Then give them a second shake in the flour bag. You'll get a thicker crust.

Fry for 4–5 minutes. Turn the quail over and fry for another 3–4 minutes. You will probably need to fry in batches, so just leave the unfried quail in the colander until you are ready to flour them up and fry them. Don't let the floured pieces sit.

When the quail are fried, let them rest on a rack set over a paper towel to drain away any excess oil. Serve hot or at room temperature with Peach Chutney.

Continued

Peach Chutney

MAKES 3 CUPS

2 teaspoons vegetable oil

1 cup finely diced red onion

1 serrano chile or jalapeño pepper, finely diced

2 tablespoons bourbon or vanilla extract

2 tablespoons lime juice

2 tablespoons balsamic reduction

2 to 3 tablespoons packed brown sugar

Kosher salt to taste

3 to 4 cups chopped peaches, divided

1 teaspoon cornstarch

2 teaspoons water

2 tablespoons chopped fresh basil

Freshly ground black pepper to taste

In a medium saucepan, heat the oil over medium heat. Add in the onion and chile pepper. Cook, stirring occasionally until softened, 2–3 minutes.

Add in the bourbon, lime juice, balsamic reduction, and brown sugar. Season with salt. Bring to a boil and immediately reduce to a simmer. Cook, stirring occasionally, 10–12 minutes. Add half of the peaches and sauté, about 2 minutes.

In a small bowl, whisk together the cornstarch and water. Add the cornstarch mixture to the pan. Stir to combine and add the rest of the peaches. Continue to gently simmer for 3–5 minutes or until the chutney is thickened to desired consistency.

Remove pan from heat and stir in basil. Taste and adjust for seasoning with salt and pepper. Allow to cool on the counter before serving, or transfer to a container, cover, and chill until ready to serve.

Balsamic Reduction

MAKES ½ CUP

2 cups good-quality balsamic vinegar

½ cup brown sugar

Heat balsamic vinegar and brown sugar in a small saucepan over medium heat. Bring to a gentle boil then reduce heat to medium low and let simmer, stirring occasionally, until the vinegar thickens and is reduced to about ½ cup, about 10 minutes. It should be thick enough to coat the back of a spoon. Remove from heat and allow to cool completely before serving.

LOUISIANA CATFISH WITH OKRA AND CORN

MAKES 4 SERVINGS

2 cups sliced okra

1¾ cups corn kernels, fresh or frozen

1 onion, diced

½ teaspoon kosher salt

3 tablespoons olive oil, divided

2 tablespoons Creole seasoning, divided

1 pound catfish fillets, patted dry and cut into
 4 portions

Preheat oven to 450 degrees.

Combine okra, corn, onion, salt, 1 tablespoon oil, and 1 tablespoon Creole seasoning in a large bowl. Spread the mixture out on a large rimmed baking sheet. Roast, stirring twice, until the vegetables are tender and beginning to brown, 20–25 minutes.

Sprinkle both sides of catfish with the remaining Creole seasoning. Heat the remaining oil in a large nonstick skillet over medium-high heat. Reduce heat to medium, add the fish and cook until just cooked through and starting to brown, about 4 minutes per side. Serve with the roasted vegetables.

SUMMERY PEACH CAKE WITH VANILLA WHIPPED CREAM AND CANE SYRUP

MAKES 8 SERVINGS

4 medium peaches*

1½ cups all-purpose flour

1½ teaspoons baking powder

½ teaspoon kosher salt

6 tablespoons butter, plus more for pan,
  room temperature

1 cup sugar

1 egg

½ cup buttermilk

2½ teaspoons vanilla extract, divided

1 tablespoon sparkling sugar, for topping

1 cup cold heavy cream

2 tablespoons powdered sugar

Cane syrup, to drizzle

Peel and slice each peach into 8 equal slices. Arrange on a paper towel–lined plate to remove some of the moisture; set aside.

Position rack in center of oven and preheat oven to 350 degrees. Generously butter 1 (9-inch) deep-dish pie pan.

In a medium bowl, whisk together flour, baking powder, and salt; set aside. In a large bowl, use an electric mixer to blend the butter until creamy. Add the sugar and beat on medium-high speed until light and fluffy. With the mixer on low, slowly blend in the egg, buttermilk, and 2 teaspoons vanilla. Then gradually mix in the flour mixture until just combined.

Scrape the batter into the prepared pie pan and smooth the top. Arrange the peach slices on top of the batter with as little space between them as possible, lightly pressing them down. Sprinkle the top of the cake with the sparkling sugar.

Bake for 10 minutes then reduce the oven temperature to 325 degrees and continue baking for 50–60 minutes, or until cake tests done with a toothpick inserted into the center of the cake. Place on a wire rack and allow to cool.

While cake is cooling, place a mixer bowl and whisk attachment in the freezer for 20 minutes to chill. Pour cream, powdered sugar, and remaining vanilla into the cold bowl and whisk on high speed until medium-to-stiff peaks form.

Slice cake into wedges and serve with fresh whipped cream and drizzle with cane syrup.

*If you can't get fresh peaches, frozen peaches can be substituted.

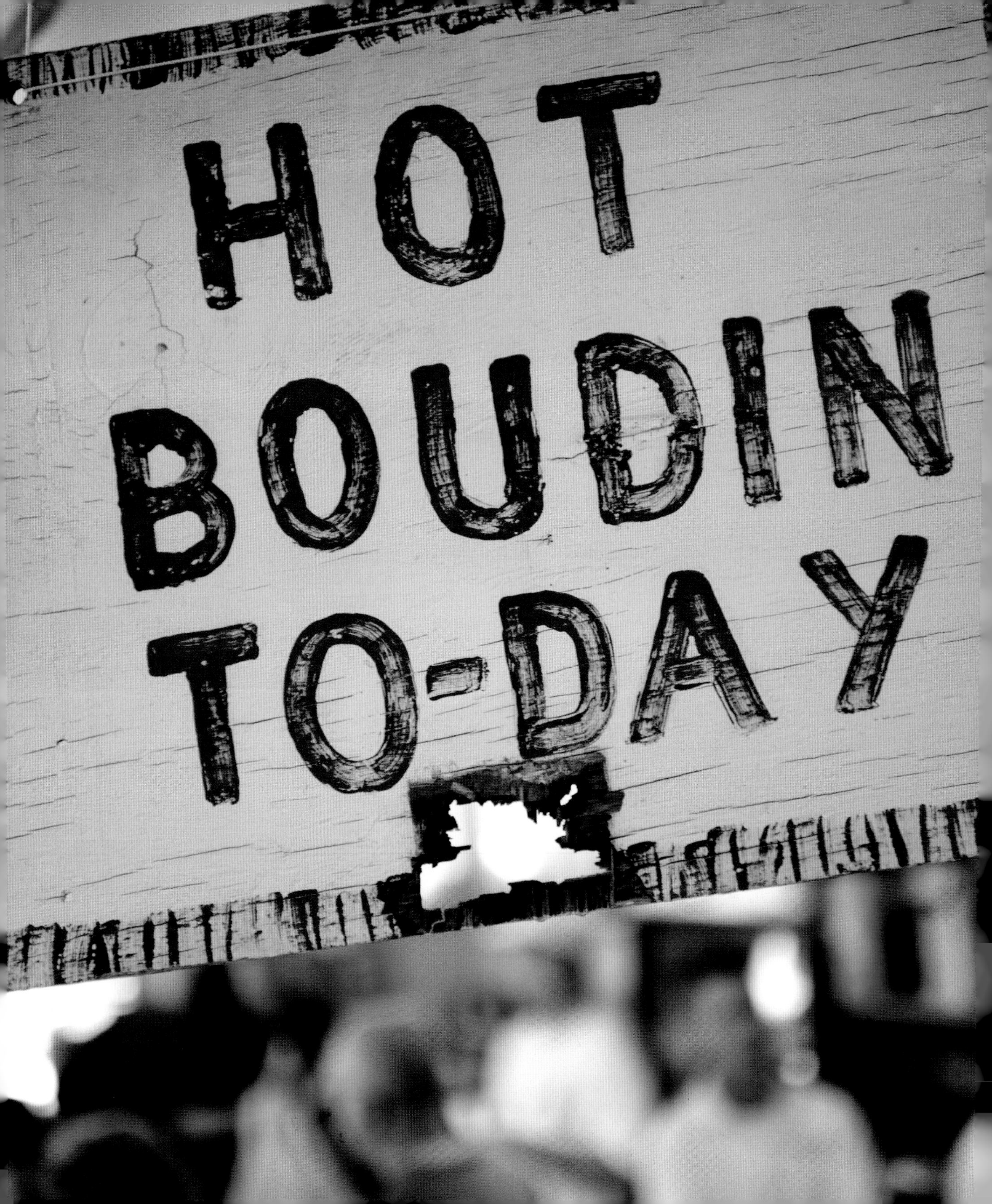
HOT
BOUDIN
TO-DAY

DELTA DELIGHTS
Northeast Louisiana

I am an LSU Tiger, but my sons Kevin and Jonathan chose to attend the University of Louisiana, Lafayette. They are Ragin' Cajuns. And Kevin played football all four years at ULL.

At one of the last games of the season one year, Kev and his teammates were taking on the University of Louisiana, Monroe, in Monroe, which is located in the Northeast corner of the state. I was there to watch the game, and before the teams took the field, I thought the stadium announcer kept saying, "Welcome to Camel Night." There was some pregame entertainment of three fans chosen at random to see who could throw a football closest to cardboard cut-outs of a deer, a turkey, and a duck. The teams came out to warm-up, and the announcer welcomed everyone again to Camel Night. I was sitting with another dad at the time, and the announcer asked everyone to welcome the

ULM president. The university president came out riding a four-wheeler, throwing t-shirts to the crowd—not how you typically imagine the leadership of a university. Both of us dads had played college football, and we were shocked to think that a cigarette company (Camel) could sponsor a university sporting event. As we talked, the other dad's wife, who was sitting behind us, leaned in and said, "Hey geniuses, he is saying CAMO and not CAMEL Night." That's when it all made sense, and when we noticed how many ULM fans were dressed in camouflage. This was the first week of hunting season.

Northeast Louisiana has beautiful wooded areas with rolling hills where you can get out and enjoy nature at its finest. Whenever I'm in the area, I think about a cold winter night in November, and giggle that I need to dress appropriately—and that means dressing in CAMO.

CHICKEN AND DUMPLINGS

MAKES 6 SERVINGS

1 tablespoon olive oil

3 stalks celery, sliced

3 carrots, diced

1 onion, diced

3 cloves garlic, minced

4 boneless chicken thighs

2 tablespoons Creole seasoning

1 teaspoon kosher salt

½ teaspoon white pepper

6 cups chicken stock

2 cups milk

1 tablespoon cornstarch

¼ cup water

Parsley, for garnish

Dumplings

2 cups all-purpose flour

½ teaspoon baking powder

1 teaspoon kosher salt

⅓ cup shortening, cold

1 cup buttermilk

Heat a large Dutch oven over medium-high heat. Add oil, celery, carrots, and onion and sauté 5 minutes, or until onion is soft and translucent. Stir in garlic and cook 1 minute more.

Add in chicken, Creole seasoning, salt, and pepper. Pour in stock and milk. Bring to a boil and boil 20 minutes, or until chicken is cooked through and easily shreds with a fork.

Meanwhile, make the dumpling dough. Mix flour, baking powder, and salt in a mixing bowl. Cut in the shortening using a pastry cutter. Gradually pour in the buttermilk, stirring until the dough comes together. Turn the dough out on a floured surface and work it just until everything is well combined. Roll the dough out to about ¼ inch thick. Cut into 1-inch strips. Cut each strip into pieces that are approximately 2 inches in length.

Remove chicken to a cutting board, shred, and return to soup. In a small bowl, whisk together cornstarch and water. Pour into soup, stir, and return to a simmer. Drop strips of dough into the soup and simmer 15–20 minutes. Garnish with parsley and serve.

WHITE BEAN SALAD

MAKES 6 SERVINGS

1 shallot, finely chopped

⅓ cup white wine vinegar

1 tablespoon Creole seasoning

½ teaspoon kosher salt

¼ cup chopped cilantro

¼ cup chopped parsley

2 tablespoons chopped mint

6 green onions, thinly sliced

⅓ cup extra virgin olive oil

2 (15-ounce) cans white beans or cannellini
    beans, drained and rinsed

1 teaspoon crushed red pepper flakes

Stir the shallot, vinegar, Creole seasoning, and salt together in a measuring cup. Set aside for 5 minutes.

In a large mixing bowl, toss together the cilantro, parsley, mint, and green onions with the oil to coat evenly. Gently toss in the beans, red pepper flakes, and the shallot-vinegar mixture to combine.

Serve immediately or store in the refrigerator for up to 5 days.

HOG'S HEAD CHEESE

MAKES 60 SERVINGS

10 cups water

2½ pounds pork roast, cubed

1 pig's foot

2 teaspoons kosher salt, divided

2 onions, chopped

1 tablespoon parsley flakes

1 tablespoon celery flakes

1 cup chopped green onions

1 tablespoon Creole seasoning

1 teaspoon black pepper

1 teaspoon red pepper

Crackers

Measure water into a 5-quart stockpot. Add pork, pig's foot, and 1 teaspoon salt. Cook, uncovered, until meat is tender and the pig's foot can easily be boned. Approximately 3 cups of liquid should remain in the pot.

Add onions, parsley, celery flakes, green onions, the remaining salt, Creole seasoning, black pepper, and red pepper. Cook for about 3 minutes.

Remove the meat, reserving the liquid. Debone the meat. Place meat in a food processor and chop well. Mix together the chopped ingredients and the reserved liquid. Pour into 2 loaf pans. Chill thoroughly.

To serve, slice into 60 (2 tablespoon-size) slices, and serve on crackers.

LOUISIANA STATE BEVERAGE
Milk Does a Dish Good

There are certain sights, smells, sounds, and tastes that trigger memories from childhood and growing up. One that I remember so well was the clink of glass bottles of milk being delivered to our house. Milk delivery in New Orleans was very popular and prevalent in the 50s and 60s. When my mom would wake up, one of the first things she did was write her order on a note, roll it up with dollar bills inside, and place the empty bottles outside on the porch with a note resting just inside the lip the bottle. In the quiet of the morning, the milkmen never had to knock because you could always here the clink of the empty bottles being replaced with full ones of chilled sweet milk. As I got older, it was my job to bring in the fresh milk and put it into the refrigerator.

Every once in a while Mom would get a bottle of chocolate milk as a treat for Dad. One morning it looked so enticing, I had to have a taste. I carefully removed the paper cap, took a few huge sips, then I realized it was gonna be noticed that the bottle wasn't full. What was a little boy to do? I ran inside with the bottle in hand, and, somehow it made sense, to fill it with water from the faucet. I carefully recapped the bottle as best as I could and quickly put the chocolate milk away in the refrigerator. Later that night, Dad poured a glass of chocolate milk, took a sip, looked at the glass, and told my mom, "Maybe I'm just tired, but it just doesn't taste the same tonight." To this day, I'm not quite sure if they ever found out what I had done, but that was the first and last time I took a taste before coming into the house. I guess guilt will do that to you.

CREOLE BLT CHEESECAKE

MAKES 24 SERVINGS

¾ cup seasoned breadcrumbs

½ cup grated Parmesan cheese

3 tablespoons butter, melted

4 (8-ounce) packages cream cheese, softened

½ cup heavy cream

1 pound bacon, cooked and crumbled

1 cup sun-dried tomatoes, patted dry and chopped

1 cup grated Gruyère cheese

3 green onions, sliced

2 tablespoons Creole seasoning

½ teaspoon kosher salt

1 teaspoon white pepper

4 large eggs, lightly beaten

Chopped cherry tomatoes and additional crumbled cooked bacon, for topping, optional

Preheat oven to 325 degrees. Place a greased 9-inch springform pan on a double thickness of heavy-duty aluminum foil. Securely wrap foil around pan.

In a small bowl, combine breadcrumbs, Parmesan cheese, and butter. Press onto the bottom of the prepared pan to make a crust. Place pan on a baking sheet and bake for 12 minutes. Cool on a wire rack.

In a large bowl, beat cream cheese and heavy cream until smooth. Beat in the bacon, sun-dried tomatoes, Gruyère cheese, green onions, Creole seasoning, salt, and pepper. Add eggs and beat on low speed just until combined. Pour over crust. Place springform pan in a large baking pan, and carefully add 1 inch of boiling water to larger pan without getting water in the cheesecake.

Bake 45–55 minutes or until center is just set and top appears dull. Remove springform pan from water bath and remove foil. Cool cheesecake on a wire rack for 10 minutes and then loosen edges from pan with a knife. Cool 1 hour longer. Refrigerate overnight.

Remove springform side from pan. Serve cheesecake with toppings if desired.

EGGNOG BREAD PUDDING

MAKES 10 TO 12 SERVINGS

Homemade Eggnog

6 large egg yolks

½ cup sugar

1 cup heavy cream

2 cups milk

½ teaspoon ground nutmeg

Pinch of salt

¼ teaspoon vanilla extract

Bread Pudding

1 (10-ounce) stale and dry loaf French bread

3 cups eggnog

4 eggs

1 teaspoon allspice

2 cups sugar

½ to 1 cup milk

1 cup butter

1 cup golden raisins

Ground cinnamon, for topping

Bread Pudding Sauce

¼ cup butter

2 cups powdered sugar

2 egg yolks

Homemade Eggnog

Whisk the egg yolks and sugar together in a medium bowl until light and creamy.

In a saucepan over medium-high heat, combine the cream, milk, nutmeg, and salt. Stir often until mixture reaches a light simmer.

Add 1 big spoonful of the hot milk to the egg mixture, whisking vigorously. Repeat, adding 1 big spoonful at a time, to temper the eggs. Once most of the hot milk has been added to the eggs, pour the mixture back into the saucepan on the stove.

Whisk constantly for a few minutes, until the mixture is just slightly thickened, or until it reaches about 160 degrees with a thermometer. Remove from heat and stir in the vanilla.

Pour the eggnog into a pitcher and cover with plastic wrap. Refrigerate until chilled. It will thicken as it cools. If you want a thinner, completely smooth consistency, you can add the entire mixture to a blender with 1 to 2 tablespoons of milk and blend until smooth. Store homemade eggnog in the refrigerator for up to 1 week.

For a tasty drink, serve with a sprinkle of cinnamon or nutmeg, and whipped cream.

Bread Pudding

Preheat oven to 350 degrees. Grease a 9 x 13-inch baking dish.

Break up French bread in a large bowl. Add eggnog and let sit for 2 minutes. Start mixing and add eggs. Stir until well mixed. Stir allspice into sugar and add. At this point the mixture should be moist, but you may need to add milk to attain the texture of oatmeal.

Melt butter over a low heat and add raisins to the butter once it has melted. Leave the butter and raisins on the heat for 2 minutes until the raisins are plump. Add the butter and raisins to the bowl and gently combine. Spoon into prepared baking dish and bake for 1–1½ hours until golden brown and the pudding has a firm texture.

Bread Pudding Sauce

Melt butter and remove from heat. Spread powdered sugar on top of the butter and place yolks on top of the sugar. Whisk together until smooth. Serve drizzled over bread pudding.

Tip: You can add about ¼ to ½ cup of your favorite liqueur, juice, or hard liquor to the sauce.

ANDOUILLE, LEEK, AND POTATO SOUP

3 tablespoons butter

1 pound andouille sausage, cubed

4 large leeks, white and light green parts only, roughly chopped

3 cloves garlic, minced

2 pounds Yukon Gold potatoes, roughly chopped into ½-inch pieces

7 cups chicken stock

½ teaspoon dried thyme

1 tablespoon Creole seasoning

1 teaspoon salt

¼ teaspoon black pepper

1 cup heavy cream

Parsley, for garnish

Melt the butter over medium heat in a large soup pot. Sauté andouille until browned, and then remove from pot with a slotted spoon and drain on paper towels. Add the leeks and garlic to the pot and cook, stirring regularly, until soft and wilted, about 10 minutes. Adjust the heat as necessary so not to brown.

Add the potatoes, stock, thyme, Creole seasoning, salt, and pepper to pot and bring to a boil. Cover and turn the heat down to low. Simmer for 15 minutes, or until the potatoes are very soft.

Purée the soup with a hand-held immersion blender until smooth. Add the heavy cream and andouille sausage and bring to a simmer. Taste and adjust seasoning if necessary. If soup is too thin, simmer until thickened. If it's too thick, add stock to thin it out. Garnish with fresh parsley.

Serve with your favorite crusty bread and top with croutons and cheese.

Homemade Croutons

MAKES 3 TO 4 CUPS

1 pound stale crusty bread, cut into cubes

½ cup vegetable oil

2 tablespoons garlic powder

2 tablespoons dried parsley

Preheat oven to 300 degrees.

Place bread cubes onto a shallow baking pan or baking sheet. Drizzle oil over the bread to lightly cover and sprinkle with garlic powder and parsley.

The baking time will depend on how big you make the bread cubes. Bake at 300 degrees until lightly brown and toasted. It won't take very long, so watch carefully.

BATON ROUGE
Red Stick Capital

Pierre Le Moyne d'Iberville left New Orleans with an exploration party up the Mississippi River in the late 1600s. Along the way, they saw a red pole that marked the boundary between Houma and Bayagoula tribal hunting grounds. In French, *le baton rouge* translates to "the red stick." This is where Baton Rouge was founded and how it got its name.

One of my first trips to Baton Rouge was when I was in elementary school, and we went on a field trip to the state capital where we visited the governor's mansion, the capital building, and the planetarium. In high school, I returned for a state choral festival competition, and then I spent years there attending LSU. There was something about the city I could not put my finger on. New Orleans has an ambience about it that just makes you feel like you could be strolling down a cobblestone street in France somewhere. Cajun Country takes you to an area that honors families of the past, keeping their heritage alive. Going north in the state, you get into farmland where a hard day's work earns you a restful night's sleep. I finally figured out that Baton Rouge doesn't have a distinct feel to it because it's a little of all of Louisiana. Being the capital city, people come to work and to live there from all over the state. And with them they bring pieces of communities near and far to create our capital city, which is a little bit of all of us.

TAPSILOG WITH SINANGAG

MAKES 4 SERVINGS

Tapsilog (Filipino Beef Tapa)

¼ cup soy sauce

¼ cup calamansi juice or lime juice

3 tablespoons brown sugar

6 cloves garlic, minced

¼ teaspoon freshly ground black pepper

1 pound New York strip or boneless rib-eye,
   thinly sliced against the grain

1 tablespoon cooking oil

Sinangag

4 fried or sunny-side-up eggs

Fresh tomato slices

Sliced cucumber

Mix together soy sauce, calamansi juice, brown sugar, garlic, and black pepper until sugar is dissolved. Toss in sliced beef. Cover and let marinate in the refrigerator for at least 4 hours or up to 24 hours.

Strain beef from marinade. Add cooking oil to a large skillet over medium heat. Once oil is hot, prepare beef in batches, cooking meat on each side for 2–4 minutes until well browned.

Serve hot with Sinangag, fried eggs, tomato slices, and cucumber.

Sinangag (Garlic Fried Rice)

MAKES 6 TO 8 SERVINGS

1 cup vegetable oil

1 cup cloves garlic, sliced paper thin

4 cups freshly cooked jasmine rice, kept hot

Kosher salt to taste

In a medium saucepan, heat the vegetable oil over medium heat until the oil begins to shimmer. Line a plate with paper towels and set it nearby.

Carefully pour the garlic into the hot oil and stir continuously until the garlic is just beginning to lightly brown. Remove the pan from the heat and use a slotted spoon to transfer the fried garlic onto the paper towel–lined plate; reserve the oil.

Fluff the hot rice with a fork and toss it with ¼ cup of the garlic oil and ½ cup of the fried garlic chips. Season the rice with salt and serve right away or at room temperature. The remaining garlic chips can be saved for future use. Store in an air-tight container in the refrigerator.

Note: You can also make Sinangag using leftover rice. Just heat the rice in a pan with 1 to 2 tablespoons garlic oil. When the rice is hot, add 2 tablespoons of the garlic and a drizzle of garlic oil.

CREOLE PORK
SAUCE PICANTE

MAKES 4 TO 6 SERVINGS

1 (4-pound) pork loin, cut ½ inch thick

1 tablespoon Creole seasoning

¼ teaspoon cayenne pepper

¼ teaspoon black pepper

½ teaspoon kosher salt

½ teaspoon paprika

½ teaspoon basil

½ teaspoon garlic powder

3 tablespoons olive oil

2 tablespoons butter

6 green onions, chopped

½ cup chopped onion

½ cup chopped green bell pepper

½ cup chopped celery

5 tablespoons all-purpose flour

1 (14-ounce) can fire-roasted tomatoes

½ teaspoon thyme

1 tablespoon chopped parsley

2 bay leaves

3 cloves garlic, minced

1 jalapeño pepper, seeded and minced

½ cup dry white wine

2½ cups beef stock

Parsley, for garnish

Cooked rice, for serving

Pound pork loin to about a ¼-inch thickness and cut into bite-size pieces.

Mix the Creole seasoning, cayenne, black pepper, salt, paprika, basil, and garlic powder together and lightly sprinkle both sides of the pork pieces.

Heat the oil in a wide heavy skillet or Dutch oven over medium heat until hot. Add the pork and brown on both sides. Remove meat and add the butter. When sizzling, add the green onions, onion, bell pepper, and celery. Sauté for 5 minutes. Stir in the flour and any remaining seasoning from the pork, and cook another 5 minutes, stirring occasionally.

Add the tomatoes with juice, thyme, parsley, bay leaves, garlic, and jalapeño. Stir in the wine and stock. Simmer for 15–25 minutes until thickened. Adjust seasoning by adding salt as needed. Add the pork, nestling into the sauce, reduce heat to low, and simmer partially covered for about 1 hour. Turn off heat and let set, covered, for 10 minutes before serving. Garnish with parsley and serve over rice.

CAPITAL MEATLOAF WITH BROWN SUGAR GLAZE

Makes 8 servings

Meat Loaf

1 teaspoon olive oil

1 cup diced onion

4 cloves garlic, minced

1 tablespoon parsley

1 egg, beaten

1/2 cup beef stock

2 ounces tomato paste

2 tablespoons sugar

1 tablespoon red wine vinegar

1 tablespoon Worcestershire sauce

1 tablespoon Creole mustard

1 tablespoon Creole seasoning

1 teaspoon kosher salt

1/2 teaspoon white pepper

2 pounds ground beef

1 1/2 cups seasoned breadcrumbs

5 bacon strips

Brown Sugar Glaze

1/4 cup black coffee

2 tablespoons whiskey

1/8 cup soy sauce

1/4 cup brown sugar

1/2 cup barbecue sauce

1/4 cup honey

1 tablespoon Worcestershire sauce

Meatloaf

Preheat oven to 350 degrees.

Add oil to a small pan and sauté the onion until translucent. Add the garlic and parsley and sauté another 30 seconds. Set aside to cool.

In a large bowl, add the egg, stock, tomato paste, sugar, vinegar, Worcestershire sauce, mustard, Creole seasoning, salt, and pepper and whisk to combine. Add the ground beef, onion and garlic mixture, and breadcrumbs. Mix thoroughly until all ingredients are combined.

Place in a loaf pan, lay strips of bacon on top, and bake for 1 1/2 hours or until internal temperature is 155–160 degrees. If loaf shrinks, carefully pour off excess oil.

Brown Sugar Glaze

Combine the coffee, whiskey, soy sauce, and brown sugar in a small saucepan over medium-low heat and reduce for 10 minutes. Add barbecue sauce, honey, and Worcestershire sauce and simmer for approximately 10 minutes until thick and glossy. Serve with meatloaf.

CAMERON AND VERMILION PARISHES
Coastal Culture

Vermilion Parish has the distinct honor of being "The Most Cajun Place on Earth," and I have seen it for myself first hand. But what exactly does that mean? Cajuns were French colonists who settled in the Canadian provinces of Nova Scotia and New Brunswick in the 1600s. The settlers named their region Acadia, and were known as Acadians. In 1713, the British took over Canada and expected all settlers to defend the British kingdom. The British demanded the Protestant religion be adopted, and that just wasn't happening. Acadians refused to cooperate, so the British seized farms, burned villages, and expelled many Acadians. Families were separated by the British, who loaded them onto ships destined to many locations. Family members were shipped from New York to the West Indies. Some were sent down south to the Louisiana territories. Many Acadians felt at home in Louisiana because of its strong French culture and Catholicism. After

time and long searches, many family members were eventually reunited in Louisiana.

The importance of family can clearly be seen in the heart of Cajun country, it is the foundation of the Cajun culture, and the family that comes to mind immediately is the Cajun Power family. Marilyn and Carroll began the Cajun Power Sauce company many years ago. They worked extremely hard to establish that company and it is still going strong today. Their three adult children, Kristie, Beau, and Coby, all still help out with the family business, and have now been joined by Spencer, the oldest grandchild. This family is the epitome of a Cajun family, and I have known them for decades. When they come to New Orleans, they let me know so I can come say hi, and when I head their way, I always try to stop by, bringing them king cake (during Mardi Gras season, of course), and getting hugs from the entire family.

BLOODY MARY-SOAKED
SHRIMP SALAD

MAKES **6** SERVINGS

⅓ cup Cajun Power Bloody Mary mix or
   Bloody Mary Mix of choice

2 tablespoons lemon juice

1½ teaspoons dry mustard

½ teaspoon kosher salt

1 teaspoon Worcestershire sauce

1 teaspoon hot sauce

¼ teaspoon black pepper

1 tablespoon prepared horseradish

½ cup canola oil

1 pound shrimp, peeled and cooked

¼ cup thinly sliced red onion

12 pickled okra pods, halved

16 grape tomatoes, halved

½ cup thinly sliced celery

Celery leaves and lemon zest, for garnish

In a medium bowl, whisk together Bloody Mary mix, lemon juice, mustard, salt, Worcestershire sauce, hot sauce, pepper, and horseradish. Add oil in a slow, steady stream, whisking constantly until combined to make a dressing.

In a medium bowl, combine shrimp, onion, okra, tomatoes, and celery with ¼ cup dressing. Place salad on a platter, and serve with additional dressing. Garnish with celery leaves and lemon zest, if desired.

SEAFOOD EGGPLANT BAKE

MAKES 6 SERVINGS

3 tablespoons olive oil

½ onion, chopped

1 red bell pepper, chopped

½ cup chopped celery

3 cloves garlic, minced

2 tablespoons Creole seasoning

1 teaspoon kosher salt

½ teaspoon white pepper

1 cup cubed tasso

2 eggplants, peeled and cubed

½ cup chicken stock

1 pound shrimp, peeled and deveined

1 cup seasoned breadcrumbs

Preheat oven to 350 degrees.

Heat the oil in a large pot over medium heat. Add the onion, bell pepper, celery, garlic, Creole seasoning, salt, and pepper. Sauté for 4–5 minutes. As the onion becomes translucent, add the tasso and continue to sauté for 1–2 minutes more. Add the eggplant, chicken stock, and shrimp. Mix thoroughly and remove from the heat.

Stir in the breadcrumbs slowly, allowing them to absorb the stock. Season with additional Creole seasoning and pepper if needed. If the overall mixture becomes too dry, add a bit more stock to moisten it.

Spread the mixture in a 3-quart casserole dish and bake for 20 minutes.

BOURBON-GLAZED
FRUITCAKE COOKIES

MAKES APPROXIMATELY 144 COOKIES

Fruitcake Cookies

3 cups all-purpose flour

1 teaspoon cinnamon

½ teaspoon baking soda

1 cup butter, room temperature

1 cup packed brown sugar

3 eggs

½ cup milk

2 tablespoons cream sherry

7 cups mixed nuts, chopped

2 cups raisins, chopped

2 cups pitted dates, chopped

1 pound candied pineapple, coarsely
    chopped

1 pound red and green candied cherries,
    chopped

Nutmeg or sugar sprinkles

Bourbon Glaze

2 cups powdered sugar

1 tablespoon milk or coconut milk

1 tablespoon melted butter

½ tablespoon vanilla extract

½ tablespoon bourbon

Fruitcake Cookies

Preheat oven to 300 degrees. Grease several baking sheets. Sift together the flour, cinnamon, and baking soda in a bowl; set aside.

Beat together the butter and brown sugar in a large mixing bowl until fluffy, about 5 minutes. Beat in the eggs, 1 at a time. Gradually beat the flour mixture into the butter mixture, alternating each addition with about 2 tablespoons of milk until all the milk is incorporated and the dough is soft. Beat in the sherry, and fold in the nuts, raisins, dates, pineapple, and cherries until thoroughly mixed. Drop the dough by rounded teaspoon onto the prepared baking sheets.

Bake until the cookies are set and the bottoms are very lightly browned, 20–30 minutes. Cool on wire racks.

Bourbon Glaze

Mix together the glaze ingredients with hand mixer on medium speed. Add more milk if you like a thinner glaze or more powdered sugar if you prefer a thicker glaze. Spoon glaze over cookies and sprinkle with nutmeg or sugar sprinkles. Allow glaze to set.

CALCASIEU PARISH
Lake Charles

Louisiana has countless festivals, and I hope to attend as many as I possibly can in this lifetime. One that I've always wanted to visit and see is in Lake Charles. It used to be called Contraband Days, but is now known as the Louisiana Pirate Festival. Story has it that one of Jean LaFitte's hideouts was Contraband Bayou. It was called that because it became his favorite place to bury contraband silver and gold. In 1957, to introduce and attract visitors to the area, a group of businessmen formed Contraband Days, which highlighted the local culture and recreational activities. What started as a one-time event has grown into a yearly festival that lasts for two weekends and has activities on both land and water. There are music venues, carnival rides, competitions, parades, and of course, food, and lots of it. And besides all of the fun, this festival also helps the community. Charitable organizations, schools, and churches all host events and activities that function as some of their major fundraisers for the year. But the best thing is that you get to dress up as a pirate and walk around saying things like "Aaaaarrrrrgggghhhh" and "Ahoy, matey!" I'll keep practicing for the day I can sail into Lake Charles and say, "Shiver me timbers."

CRAB BEIGNETS

MAKES 4 SERVINGS

1 cup all-purpose flour

¼ cup cornstarch, plus 2 tablespoons more

1 tablespoon baking powder

½ teaspoon kosher salt

1 cup ginger ale

½ cup crabmeat, picked through for shells

½ cup mascarpone cheese

¼ cup chopped chives

1 shallot, finely diced

1 tablespoon Creole seasoning

2 teaspoons salt

Pinch of pepper

Vegetable oil, for frying

Combine flour, cornstarch, baking powder, and salt in a bowl. Slowly add ginger ale until batter is just thicker than pancake batter. Set aside, covered, at room temperature for up to 2 hours.

Mix together crabmeat, cheese, chives, shallot, Creole seasoning, salt, and pepper in a bowl, and then form into ½-ounce balls, about the size of a ping pong ball.

Heat oil in a fryer or cast iron skillet to 375 degrees. Gently drop crabmeat balls into the batter and lift out with a teaspoon. Carefully place them into the oil and fry for 2-3 minutes until golden brown and hot all the way through. Remove from oil and drain on paper towels.

SHRIMP AND CRAWFISH ROLL

MAKES 4 SERVINGS

1 pound cooked shrimp

1 pound crawfish tail meat, drained

2 green onions, chopped

1 stalk celery, chopped

¼ cup mayonnaise

3 tablespoons garlic sauce

½ teaspoon lemon zest

1 tablespoon fresh lemon juice

½ teaspoon chopped parsley

½ teaspoon chopped thyme

1 tablespoon Creole seasoning

1 teaspoon kosher salt

4 hot dog buns or hoagie rolls, split

2 tablespoons butter, melted

Fresh parsley leaves, for garnish

In a large bowl, gently combine shrimp and crawfish. In a small bowl, add green onions, celery, mayonnaise, garlic sauce, lemon zest and juice, parsley, thyme, Creole seasoning, and salt, mixing well. Pour over the shrimp and crawfish, stirring to make sure all is coated. Taste, and adjust seasoning if necessary. Cover shrimp mixture and refrigerate until chilled, about 30 minutes.

Brush interior of buns with melted butter. In a large skillet over medium heat, add buns, butter side down, and cook until lightly browned. Divide shrimp mixture evenly between buns, and serve garnished with parsley, if desired.

SPICY RED BEAN DIP WITH HERB FLATBREAD CRACKERS

SERVES 4

Spicy Red Bean Dip
MAKES 2 CUPS

2 cloves garlic

¼ red onion

2 spring onions

¼ cup flat-leaf parsley

¼ cup cilantro

1 tablespoon Creole seasoning

½ teaspoon kosher salt

1 teaspoon nutmeg

1 jalapeño pepper, seeded

1 tablespoon tomato paste

2 tablespoons olive oil

1 (14-ounce) can red kidney beans, drained

2 tablespoons lime juice

In a food processor, roughly blend garlic, onions, parsley, cilantro, Creole seasoning, salt, nutmeg, jalapeño, tomato paste, and oil. Add kidney beans and pulse until combined. Add lime juice until desired consistency is reached.

Herb Flatbread Crackers
MAKES 4 LARGE CRACKERS

1½ cups all-purpose flour

1 teaspoon fresh thyme

2 cloves garlic, minced

½ teaspoon freshly ground black pepper

1 teaspoon salt

1 teaspoon sugar

2 tablespoons olive oil

½ cup cold water

Preheat oven to 450 degrees. Pulse the flour, thyme, garlic, pepper, salt, sugar, and oil in a food processor until evenly distributed.

Add the water and pulse just until the dough starts to stick together, about 10–15 seconds. Remove the dough, press together gently with your hands to form a single ball, and cut into 4 pieces. Let the dough rest for about 10 minutes.

Roll out each individual piece of dough as thin as you possibly can. If the dough starts to shrink up, let it rest a little longer. You want the dough to get very, very thin. Once all 4 pieces are rolled out, place them on a piece of parchment paper and transfer to a baking sheet.

Bake for 4–5 minutes, but check periodically to make sure the pieces are not getting too brown. Flip each cracker piece and bake another 4–5 minutes. Turn the oven off and let the crackers sit in the oven for 1–2 hours to really dry out and get crispy. Break into several pieces to serve.

FISHERMAN'S PARADISE

I grew up with avid fishermen, so I'm not surprised it continues to run in the family. Even as teens, Kevin and Jonathan would walk a block to Lake Ponchartrain to fish after their homework was done. In recent years, Lenny Delbert Sr. and I have fished whenever we the time. Lenny is a cameraman on my shows, an incredible editor, and a wonderful friend to Monica and me.

Normally, it's just the two of us headed out to different spots, enjoying the weather while on the hunt for redfish, speckled trout, flounder, sheepshead, bass, sac-a-lait, catfish, and pretty much anything biting. Recently, Lenny, Lenny Jr, and his kids Graycen and Holden spent a day with me on the water with Captain Mike out of Yscloskey. We were able to fill the boat with redfish, sheepshead, and a few speckled trout. That was a fun day of fishing that produced results. Normally Lenny and I return home with only a full belly from lunch and any leftover bait. His wife Joanie says that more fish die crossing the road than we ever catch. Monica must think the same thing because she always has tasty treats waiting for our return and something prepared for Lenny to take home for dinner.

Louisiana is a state full of beautiful lakes and bayous teaming with tasty species of fish that we have seen others catch, just not usually us. But who can complain about a sunny day spent with a friend in a great setting? Now I know why it's called fishing and not catching. I guess when we're ready to catch, we'll have to call our friend Captain Mike Helmstetter to take us out to his special spot.

CRAB AU GRATIN

MAKES 6 SERVINGS

½ cup butter

1 onion, finely chopped

1 stalk celery, finely chopped

2 green onions, sliced

2 cloves garlic, minced

2 egg yolks, slightly beaten

1 (12-ounce) can evaporated milk

2 tablespoons all-purpose flour

1 lemon, zested and juiced

1 teaspoon hot sauce

1 teaspoon Worcestershire sauce

1 teaspoon Creole seasoning

1 teaspoon kosher salt

½ teaspoon cayenne pepper

½ teaspoon white pepper

½ cup grated Gruyère cheese, divided

½ cup grated fontina cheese, divided

1 pound lump crabmeat, picked for shells

Green onions, for garnish

Crackers, for serving

Preheat oven to 350 degrees.

Melt the butter in a large skillet over medium-high heat. Add the onion, celery, green onions, and garlic, and cook, stirring, until the vegetables are softened, about 5 minutes.

While the vegetables cook, whisk the egg yolks and evaporated milk together in a small bowl until well blended; set aside.

Add the flour to the skillet, and blend well into the vegetables to create a white roux, about 2 minutes. Add the milk mixture, stirring constantly to blend into the roux mixture. Stir in the lemon zest and juice, hot sauce, Worcestershire sauce, Creole seasoning, salt, cayenne, and white pepper, and continue to stir for another 4–5 minutes. If sauce seems too thick, add a little milk to thin. Remove from the heat, and fold in half the cheeses; blend until totally melted and fully incorporated.

Gently divide the crabmeat among 4 mini oven-proof casserole dishes, trying not to break up the crab lumps. Or, pour into 1 large cast iron skillet, or an 8-inch baking dish.

Pour the cheese sauce over the crab, and then sprinkle the remaining cheeses on top. Bake until bubbly, about 15 minutes, then broil until the cheese begins to brown, about 5 minutes.

Remove from the oven, garnish with the green onions and serve with crackers.

REDFISH MORNAY

MAKES 6 SERVINGS

6 redfish fillets

1 tablespoon Creole seasoning

4 tablespoons butter

⅓ cup all-purpose flour

1 cup milk

1 cup chicken stock

½ teaspoon mustard powder

¼ teaspoon kosher salt

½ teaspoon white pepper

¼ teaspoon ground nutmeg

1 cup grated cheddar cheese, divided

½ cup fresh breadcrumbs

Parsley, for garnish

Preheat oven to 350 degrees. Spray a baking dish that is large enough for a single layer of redfish with cooking oil.

Sprinkle the redfish with the Creole seasoning and cook—steam, bake, or fry until done. Place in a single layer on the bottom of the prepared baking dish.

Melt the butter in a medium pan over low heat, stir in the flour until a paste forms, and slowly add the milk while stirring continuously.

Mix together the stock, mustard, salt, pepper, and nutmeg. Add to the pan and stir until smooth then simmer 2-3 minutes until the sauce has thickened. Remove from heat.

Add in ¾ cup of the cheddar cheese, stir until melted and smooth, and then pour over the redfish. Combine the remaining cheese and breadcrumbs then sprinkle over the sauce and bake 15-20 minutes until bubbly and golden. Garnish with parsley and serve.

SEAFOOD AND CORN CASSEROLE

MAKES 8 SERVINGS

2 ½ cups corn kernels

1 (15-ounce) can creamed corn

1 (8-ounce) package corn muffin mix

½ cup sliced green onions

1 cup sour cream

½ cup butter, melted

½ pound shrimp, peeled and deveined

½ pound crabmeat, picked for shells

1 tablespoon Creole seasoning

1 teaspoon kosher salt

½ cup grated white cheddar cheese

Preheat oven to 350 degrees. Lightly grease a 9 x 13-inch casserole dish.

In a large bowl, mix together corn, creamed corn, muffin mix, green onions, sour cream, and butter. Place shrimp and crabmeat in a small bowl and season with Creole seasoning and salt. Gently mix to spread the seasonings, and add to the corn mixture.

Pour into baking dish and bake for 45 minutes, or until golden brown. Remove from oven and top with cheese. Return to oven for 5–10 minutes, or until cheese is melted. Allow to stand for 5 minutes then serve while warm.

RIVER PARISHES
Côte des Allemands

In Louisiana, you can catch catfish any time of year. There are a plethora of types, including channel, flathead, and blue catfish and they can be found in rivers, lakes, ponds, bayous, and pretty much anywhere there is water deep enough you can drop a line.

Once when my dad and I were driving on River Road, which is adjacent to the Mississippi River, he noticed a group of men staring into the trunk of a car with fishing poles in hand. My dad was eagerly asking if they had caught anything as the men pridefully smiled and just pointed into the trunk. In that trunk was the biggest fish I had ever seen to this day. They said it weighed EIGHTY pounds. I knew catfish could range anywhere from just under one pound to a hundred pounds, but I had never seen one this big.

Des Allemands has the title of being the Catfish Capital of the World, and the community has celebrated catfish with a festival since 1975. Aquatic farming has been around for many, many years and most people in the United States eat farm-raised catfish. The catfish that come from Lake Des Allemands are wild and are some of the best catfish I have ever tasted. When you eat as much catfish as I do, you know the difference between wild-caught and farm-raised (as well as the difference between fresh and frozen). I don't know if it is because the water is shallow, averaging about five feet, or because of the location of the lake, which is fed by waters from Grand Bayou and Bayou Chevreuil. But what I do know is that all the elements contribute to some of the most delicious catfish you will ever eat in your life. There is nothing like ending the day sitting out back at Spahr's Restaurant with a platter of catfish and watching the pelicans and egrets strolling by and spotting alligators gracefully moving through the bayou.

ANDOUILLE AND SHRIMP LASAGNA ROLL-UPS

MAKES 6 SERVINGS

1¼ pounds shrimp, peeled and deveined

1 onion, chopped

2 tablespoons olive oil

4 Roma tomatoes, seeded and chopped

2 tablespoons Creole seasoning

½ teaspoon kosher salt

3 cloves garlic, minced

¼ cup butter, cubed

¼ cup all-purpose flour

2 cups milk

1½ cups grated cheddar cheese

1 cup diced andouille sausage

12 lasagna noodles, cooked and drained

1 cup grated pepper jack cheese

1 teaspoon paprika

Parsley and green onions, for garnish

Preheat oven to 350 degrees. Grease a 9 x 13-inch baking dish.

In a large skillet, sauté shrimp and onion in oil until shrimp barely turn pink. Remove from heat and stir in tomatoes, Creole seasoning, and salt; set aside.

In a large saucepan, sauté garlic in butter for 1 minute. Stir in flour until blended. Gradually add milk. Bring to a boil over medium heat; cook and stir for 2 minutes until thickened. Remove from the heat; stir in cheddar cheese until smooth. Add sausage; set aside.

Spread ⅓ cup shrimp mixture over each noodle. Carefully roll up and then place seam side down in the prepared baking dish. Top with cheese sauce. Sprinkle with pepper jack cheese and paprika.

Cover and bake for 15 minutes. Uncover and then bake 10–15 minutes longer or until bubbly. Let stand 15 minutes before serving. Garnish with parsley and green onions.

CHICKEN MADEIRA

1 pound asparagus

6 cups water

1 tablespoon salt

3 tablespoons butter, divided

2 tablespoons olive oil, divided

16 ounces mushrooms, thickly sliced

1 cup finely diced onion

3 cloves garlic, minced

3 tablespoons Creole seasoning, divided

2 tablespoons chopped fresh parsley

2 chicken breasts

1½ cups Madeira wine

1½ cups beef stock

½ cup heavy cream

1 teaspoon kosher salt

½ teaspoon ground black pepper

1 cup grated mozzarella cheese

Parsley, for garnish

Remove fibrous stems from asparagus. Fill a medium pot with the water, bring to a boil, and add 1 tablespoon salt. Add asparagus and boil, uncovered, until crisp tender and bright green, 2–3 minutes, then remove from hot water and set aside.

Place a large heavy pan over medium-high heat and melt in 2 tablespoons butter and 1 tablespoon oil. Add mushrooms and cook 5 minutes until soft. Stir in onion and cook 3 minutes. Add garlic then season with 1 tablespoon Creole seasoning and parsley. Cook another 2 minutes then remove mixture to a plate.

Slice chicken breasts in half lengthwise and pound each cutlet between plastic wrap until no more than ¼ inch thick. Season chicken all over with remaining Creole seasoning. Place same pan over medium-high heat and add remaining butter and remaining oil. When butter is melted, add chicken breasts and sauté 3– 4 minutes per side or until golden and cooked through. Remove chicken from pan to the same plate with mushrooms.

In the same pan, add Madeira and boil until reduced by half, scraping the bottom of the pan to deglaze. Add stock and boil about 10 minutes, until ⅔ cup of liquid remains. Reduce heat to medium, add cream and simmer until sauce thickens. Season with salt and pepper.

Return chicken to the pan, turning it to coat in the sauce. Top with mushrooms, asparagus, and mozzarella cheese. Broil 3–4 minutes or until cheese is melted. Remove from oven, garnish with fresh parsley.

FRIED DES ALLEMANDS CATFISH WITH HOMEMADE DIPPING SAUCE

MAKES 4 TO 6 SERVINGS

Dipping Sauce

½ cup mayonnaise

2 tablespoons Creole mustard

1 tablespoon lime juice

1 tablespoon honey

1 teaspoon firmly packed brown sugar

½ teaspoon dry mustard

½ teaspoon Worcestershire sauce

½ teaspoon garlic sauce

½ teaspoon hot sauce

½ teaspoon kosher salt

Catfish

6 catfish fillets

2 tablespoons Creole seasoning

2 tablespoons kosher salt, divided

½ teaspoon cayenne pepper

1 teaspoon garlic powder

1 cup all-purpose flour

½ cup cornstarch

2 eggs, beaten

¼ cup milk

1 cup yellow cornmeal

Oil, for frying

Lemon wedges, for serving

Dipping Sauce

Place the mayonnaise, mustard, lime juice, honey, brown sugar, mustard, Worcestershire sauce, garlic sauce, hot sauce, and salt in a medium bowl.

Whisk until all the ingredients are thoroughly incorporated. Adjust seasonings to your taste and refrigerate until ready to use.

Catfish

Cut the catfish into bite-size pieces; set aside.

In a small bowl, combine Creole seasoning, 1 tablespoon salt, cayenne, and garlic powder. Mix well and sprinkle over catfish to season.

Using 3 separate dishes, combine flour, cornstarch, and remaining salt in one. Mix eggs and milk in the next, and cornmeal in the last.

Preheat oil to 350 degrees.

Dip catfish in the flour, then the egg wash, and finally into the cornmeal, shaking off excess. Fry in batches until the catfish bites are golden, 3-4 minutes.

Place the cooked catfish on a paper towels to drain, and repeat for the remaining catfish. Serve with lemon wedges and dipping sauce.

SENSATIONAL SEAFOOD
Louisiana's Crowning Glory

I was so spoiled as a child! My grandmothers and mom were fantastic cooks who made meals look effortless. I remember asking Mom what was for dinner, and after she told me, responding, "Seafood again?" When you live in an area with so many lakes, bayous, and rivers, it's no wonder you eat shrimp, fish, crawfish, and oysters at most meals. Meat made an appearance at our table two or maybe three times a week in the form of veal, roast chicken, rump roast, or pork chops. To this day, it surprises Monica that I will cook a roast or grill a steak for her and Noah and I won't eat any of it.

One of my funniest memories is about oysters on a Saturday. My mom would often make seafood po'boys for Saturday dinner. She would usually make enough for family who would stop by around dinnertime, but on this particular day, no one was coming, so she only prepared enough for the four of us (Mom, Dad, Nan, and me). While she was preparing the oysters for frying, a church friend of my grandmother's came over, and of course Mom invited her to stay for dinner. No sooner than she said yes, the doorbell rang again, and another friend of my grandmother's showed up just in time to eat. At this point, Mom had given us "the look." Without saying a word, she conveyed that my dad's and my dinner would be delayed. As I helped my mom get ready, I saw Dad walking past the kitchen window, and wondered why he was outside. Well, five minutes later, I saw him walk by again, headed toward the back door. I went to meet him, and he gave me a smile and a shrug of his shoulders, saying "You do what you gotta do." Mom had somehow signaled to Dad, and he walked up to the seafood market for more oysters. I think Dad disconnected the doorbell on his return so we could enjoy our po'boys.

CRAB CAKES

MAKES 4 SERVINGS

1 tablespoon Creole mustard

1 large egg

½ cup mayonnaise

1 lemon, zested and 1 tablespoon juice

½ small red onion, chopped

1 red bell pepper, chopped

1 tablespoon chopped cilantro

1 tablespoon Creole seasoning

1 teaspoon kosher salt

½ teaspoon cayenne pepper

1 cup seasoned breadcrumbs, divided

1 pound lump crabmeat

½ cup butter

Mixed baby greens

Lemon Vinaigrette

Parsley, for garnish

Preheat oven to 375 degrees.

In a large bowl, whisk together the mustard, egg, mayonnaise, and lemon zest and juice until smooth. Stir in the onion, bell pepper, cilantro, Creole seasoning, salt, and cayenne. Gently but thoroughly fold in ¾ cup of the breadcrumbs and the crabmeat. Place the remaining breadcrumbs in a shallow bowl.

Portion out and form the crabmeat mixture into 16 round cakes, about 2 inches tall and 2 inches wide. Dredge each crab cake in the remaining breadcrumbs just to coat lightly and place on a platter.

Line a large baking sheet with parchment paper and dust lightly with breadcrumbs.

Place a large sauté pan over medium heat and add butter. Sauté the crab cakes in batches for about 1 minute, until golden brown. As they are finished, transfer to the prepared baking sheet. When all the crab cakes have been browned, finish cooking them in the hot oven for 5 minutes.

To serve toss baby greens with Lemon Vinaigrette, divide between plates, and top with crab cakes. Garnish with parsley.

Lemon Vinaigrette

MAKES ¾ CUP

½ cup olive oil

3 tablespoons lemon juice

1 lemon, zested

1 green onion, thinly sliced

1½ teaspoons Creole mustard

½ teaspoon sugar

Pinch of kosher salt and pepper

In a bowl, whisk together oil, lemon juice, lemon zest, green onion, Creole mustard, and sugar. Season with salt and pepper. Extra dressing can be refrigerated and brought to room temperature before serving.

BAKED LOUISIANA
OYSTER CASSEROLE

MAKES **12** TO **15** SERVINGS

2 quarts oysters, drained

½ cup finely chopped parsley

½ cup finely chopped shallots

2 tablespoons Creole seasoning

1 teaspoon kosher salt

2 tablespoons hot sauce

2 tablespoons Worcestershire sauce

2 tablespoons lemon juice

½ cup butter, melted

2 cups seasoned breadcrumbs

Paprika

¾ cup half-and-half

Preheat oven to 375 degrees. Grease a shallow 2-quart baking dish.

Layer half of oysters in the bottom of prepared baking dish. Sprinkle with half of each of the parsley, shallots, Creole seasoning, salt, hot sauce, Worcestershire sauce, lemon juice, butter, and breadcrumbs. Make another layer of the same. Sprinkle with paprika.

Just before baking, pour the half-and-half into evenly spaced holes, being very careful not to moisten breadcrumb topping. Bake about 30 minutes or until firm.

PILLOWCASE COOKIES

MAKES ABOUT 24 COOKIES

2 cups all-purpose flour

1 cup raw unrefined sugar

1 tablespoon baking powder

½ teaspoon kosher salt

½ cup butter

2 eggs

1 teaspoon vanilla extract

In a food processor, combine the flour, sugar, baking powder, and salt. Pulse to mix well. Add the butter and pulse for 30 seconds. Add the eggs and vanilla and pulse until the dough comes together. Wrap in plastic wrap and refrigerate for 30 minutes.

Preheat oven to 375 degrees. Line 2 baking sheets with silicone baking mats or parchment paper.

Transfer the dough to a clean, lightly floured work surface. Using a rolling pin, roll out the dough to a ¼-inch thickness and cut it into the shapes you desire. Dip the cookie cutter in flour first, then press it into the dough. Transfer the cookies to the prepared baking sheets.

Bake for about 15 minutes, until the edges are golden brown. Remove from the oven and let cool on the pan for 2 minutes. Then transfer cookies to a wire rack and let them cool completely. These cookies are great for up to a week; store them in an airtight container at room temperature.

PICK-YOUR-OWN
Louisiana's Family Friendly Farms

The concept of you-pick farms is a wonderful piece to the larger farm-to-table puzzle. It is such a simple concept, and has so many benefits for the farmer, the picker, the economy, and our earth. Direct sales lower operating costs for the farmer, no transportation costs help everyone, and if the pickers bring their own containers, there are reduced packaging costs and wastes. The farmer also has cash in hand. The best part of you-pick farms, at least in my opinion, is that often you get to taste what you are picking so you know how good it is. And you get to see exactly where and how your food is grown and produced.

And as child, I remember picking mirliton. They are very plentiful in New Orleans when in season. If you are lucky, you own a Meyer lemon or citrus tree, or if a neighbor or a friend has a tree, hopefully they allow you to pick some fruit, or even better, they bring you some. We also have Asian pears, also known as loquat. Monica had never heard of or tasted them. One day as we were walking our rescue dog Cookie Monster, we met a lovely lady who had a tree, and in conversation with her, we told her Monica had never tried them. She encouraged us to give one a try, and to grab a few every time we walk past her house. Now every time we are out for a walk past her house, we grab just one each to enjoy. Talk about a you-pick farm! This is the Louisiana life I love so much.

PUMPKIN SOUP

2 tablespoons vegetable oil

1 onion, chopped

1 pound smoked sausage, cubed

6 cups chicken stock

2 cloves garlic, minced

1 tablespoon Creole seasoning

1 tablespoon ground cumin

2 teaspoons dried oregano

2 (15-ounce) cans white beans, rinsed and
   drained

2 cups pumpkin, fresh or canned

1 cup Rotel tomatoes

½ teaspoon kosher salt

5 cups fresh spinach

Croutons, for garnish

In a 6-quart stockpot, heat oil and sauté onion until tender. Add sausage and sauté until slightly browned. Add stock, garlic, Creole seasoning, cumin, and oregano and bring to a boil.

Stir in beans, pumpkin, Rotel tomatoes, and salt until combined and return to a boil. Reduce heat, simmer uncovered for about 20 minutes, and stir occasionally.

Stir in spinach and cook until wilted, 3–5 minutes. Serve topped with croutons, if desired.

Fresh Pumpkin

MAKES 3 TO 6 CUPS

1 (4 to 6 pound) pie pumpkin

½ teaspoon salt

Preheat oven to 375 degrees.

Slice pumpkin in half and scoop out the seeds and strings. Salt both halves and place, cut side down, onto a baking sheet lined with aluminum foil or parchment paper. Roast for 40–60 minutes or until tender. Remove from oven and allow to cool. When cool, scrape flesh from the skin. Using a food processor, purée pumpkin flesh until smooth.

CHANTILLY CAKE

Cake

3 cups cake flour

2 teaspoons baking powder

1 teaspoon kosher salt

2 cups plain Greek yogurt

4 eggs

1 teaspoon vanilla extract

1 cup canola oil

1 lemon, zested and juiced

1½ cups sugar

Whipped Topping

1 cup cold heavy cream

1 cup powdered sugar, sifted

1 cup mascarpone, room temperature

3 cups fresh berries of choice

Preheat oven to 350 degrees and grease and line 3 (8-inch) round cake pans with parchment paper.

Sift together the flour, baking powder, and salt and set aside. In a separate bowl, combine the yogurt, eggs, vanilla, oil, and lemon zest and juice, and then stir in the sugar and mix well.

Add the wet ingredients into the dry ingredients and mix to combine.

Pour the batter into the prepared cake pans and bake for 25–30 minutes or until a toothpick inserted comes out clean. Remove from the oven and allow to cool before turning out onto a wire rack. Make sure the layers are completely cool before assembling the cake.

To make the topping, slowly whip the cream with the powdered sugar until soft peaks form. Add the mascarpone and whip to stiff peaks.

To assemble the cake, sandwich the cake layers together with the whipped cream and berries. Save some berries to decorate the top of the cake. Serve immediately.

BLUEBERRY-CUSTARD PIE

MAKES 8 SERVINGS

1½ cups sugar

1 cup buttermilk

3 large eggs

2 tablespoons butter, melted

1 teaspoon vanilla extract

½ cup all-purpose flour

¼ teaspoon kosher salt

1½ cups fresh blueberries or frozen
    blueberries, thawed

1 (9-inch) pie crust, unbaked (page 83)

Preheat oven to 350 degrees.

In a large bowl, add the sugar, buttermilk, eggs, butter, and vanilla. Whisk until well combined. Add the flour and salt. Whisk until no dry flour remains. Add the blueberries. Gently stir until well incorporated.

Place the pie crust in a 9-inch pie pan. Pour the pie filling into the pie crust. Bake for 50 minutes. Cool at room temperature for 1 hour. Then refrigerate for at least 2 hours before serving.

PLAQUEMINES PARISH
Louisiana Citrus

Venice, Louisiana, sits at the bottom right of the state. When you look at Louisiana, it is shaped like a boot and Venice sits at the toe where the Mississippi River flows into the Gulf of Mexico. I have often taken a ride with a friend when he'd travel there to purchase seafood for his company. On the drive, as soon as we entered Plaquemines Parish, I would see fruit stands and citrus orchards. Oranges, satsumas, kumquats, grapefruit, tangerines, mandarins, lemons, and limes are grown in abundance there, with each tree receiving a little tender love and care. It's no secret my favorite are lemons, probably because I remember Mom always making lemonade, and I would grab a couple lemon slices dipped in sugar as a treat.

A fellow Kiwanian knew my love of lemons, and would bring me grocery bags full of Meyer lemons from her tree. She told me that her tree produced over 300 lemons one year. So I had to join the growing party. I purchased two lemon trees along with a navel orange and a lime tree, hoping to reap the benefits in years to come. I know it takes patience, and I'm in it for the long haul. After talking to my trees every day and making sure their thirst was quenched, we had our first harvest—three lemons from one tree, one lemon from the other, and as for the orange and lime trees, nothing. Monica said the lemon tree with one lonely lemon looked like our very own Charlie Brown Christmas Tree. I'm gonna try to be good and stay on the nice list, and maybe Old St. Nick will give me more to pick this upcoming growing season.

BAKED CHICKEN
WITH SATSUMA GLAZE

MAKES 4 SERVINGS

1 pound boneless chicken thighs or breasts

2 tablespoons Creole seasoning

1 cup all-purpose flour

1 tablespoon smoked paprika

2 teaspoons kosher salt

1½ tablespoons olive oil

4 satsumas, juiced with some pulp

1 orange, zested

1 tablespoon brown sugar

Preheat oven to 350 degrees. If the pieces of chicken are more than ½ inch thick, place them between sheets of plastic wrap and pound thinner. Sprinkle chicken with Creole seasoning. Combine the flour, paprika, and salt in a flat-bottom bowl or pan. Drop each piece of chicken in the flour and flip to coat well.

Heat the oil over medium-high heat in a large flat skillet. Place each piece of chicken in the oil and brown for about 2 minutes on each side. Remove the chicken and place in a 9 x 13-inch baking pan. Pour the citrus juice in the hot skillet and stir to deglaze, scraping up all the browned bits. Pour this mixture over the chicken. Sprinkle with the zest and the brown sugar. Bake for 30 minutes.

CHARGRILLED OYSTERS

MAKES 4 SERVINGS

2 cups butter, divided

2 bunches green onions, finely chopped

20 cloves garlic, puréed

1 teaspoon crushed red pepper

3 tablespoons finely chopped thyme

3 tablespoons finely chopped oregano

2 tablespoons lemon juice

1 tablespoon Worcestershire sauce

2 tablespoons Creole seasoning

¼ cup white wine

24 oysters, freshly shucked (on the half shell)

8 ounces Romano cheese, grated

1 loaf French bread

The butter-garlic sauce should be prepared just prior to grilling the oysters. In a large sauté pan, add 1 cup butter and place over medium heat. Melt the butter and bring to a simmer. Add green onions, garlic, red pepper, thyme, oregano, lemon juice, Worcestershire sauce, and Creole seasoning. Cook for 2 minutes and add white wine. Stir ingredients continuously and cook until green onions are soft. Remove from heat and allow to cool for 3 minutes.

In a large mixing bowl, before mixture is completely cool, combine the remaining butter with the sauce. Blend until butter is melted and folded into the sauce. Final product should have a creamy consistency.

Grilling Oysters

Preheat grill to 350 degrees. Once at temperature, place shucked oysters on the half shell on the center of the grill. Once the water around the oyster begins to bubble and the oyster begins to rise, ladle 1 tablespoon of the butter-garlic sauce on top of each oyster. Make sure that the sauce is well blended. This insures the proper blend of butter and seasoning. Oysters should brown slightly around the edges. Top with a sprinkle cheese and allow the cheese to melt. Remove oysters and place on a heat-resistant plate or platter. Serve immediately with warm French bread for dipping.

SATSUMA CAKE

MAKES 6 TO 8 SERVINGS

½ cup butter, plus 1 tablespoon more, room
   temperature, divided

½ cup sugar, plus 5 tablespoons more,
   divided

6 to 8 satsumas, depending on the size

1½ cups all-purpose flour

1½ teaspoons baking powder

½ teaspoon kosher salt

1 egg

2 teaspoons vanilla extract

¾ cup milk

Preheat oven to 350 degrees. Grease 1 (9-inch) round cake pan with 1 tablespoon butter then sprinkle 2 tablespoons sugar evenly across the bottom of the pan.

Peel the satsumas. Place whole satsumas on their side with segments parallel to a cutting board and slice each into 3 even sections.

Arrange the sliced satsumas in cake pan. Start at the center and work out, ensuring the entire surface of the pan in covered in pieces. After arranging full slices in your pan, you can cut the remaining slices into smaller pieces in order to fill any gaps.

With a stand or hand mixer, cream ½ cup butter and ½ cup plus 3 tablespoons sugar for 4–6 minutes on medium speed, scraping down the sides of the mixing bowl as needed. When creamed, the mixture will have a light and fluffy texture.

In a separate bowl, combine flour, baking powder, and salt together; set aside. Add the egg to the creamed butter and sugar mixture and combine. Add the vanilla extract.

Add ½ of the flour mixture, then ½ of the milk and combine. Add the rest of the flour, then the rest of the milk and mix until just combined.

Use a spatula to gently finish mixing as not to overmix the batter. Pour batter into the cake pan over the satsuma pieces, being careful to not disturb and move the satsumas. Use a spatula to spread the batter and then tap the cake pan lightly on the counter several times to help even out the batter.

Place on the middle rack in the oven and bake for 50–60 minutes. A toothpick inserted should come out clean and the cake should have an even, golden appearance.

Let to cool for 5 minutes. After 5 minutes run a knife around the edges of the pan then place a plate or wire rack on top of the cake pan and invert the cake upside down. The cake should fall out of the pan within 30 seconds of being upside down. If it doesn't, you can lightly tap the bottom of the pan to help it along.

FLORIDA PARISHES
Cultural Crossroads

Madisonville is "across the lake" from New Orleans. That's across Lake Ponchatrain. Ms. Leah Chase is from Madisonville, and around these parts, she doesn't need a last name. If you say Ms. Leah, just about everyone knows who you are talking about.

Ms. Leah did so many wonderful things in her lifetime. I could write a whole book about those things, but this is about knowing her personally. I have fond memories from childhood about going to her restaurant, Dooky Chase, and seeing Ms. Leah. I guess you could say I have known her my whole life. Ms. Leah was the sweetest lady that you would ever know, BUT, she would also tell you how it is. We lost Ms. Leah in 2019, an unimaginable loss.

I introduced Monica to Ms. Leah when she first moved here. Ms. Leah embraced her in true Ms. Leah style. From then on, Monica would say, "Ms. Leah is of a certain age and it wouldn't be a surprise if we woke up tomorrow and she was gone." We would go see Ms. Leah every couple of weeks. We would sneak in the back, and sometimes bring her flowers. We would see how she was doing, and ask about the family and the restaurant.

On one visit to see Ms. Leah, she pulled me aside and said, "Kevin, I have never seen you look better. I have never seen you happier or healthier. Kevin, I have never seen you more successful. It's about time you make a real commitment to this girl, young man." At the time I was almost sixty years old and a grandfather. And that was Ms. Leah telling it how it is. That memory always makes Monica giggle. What she didn't know at the time was that Monica and I had planned a surprise wedding a few months later and she was invited.

On another cherished visit to see Ms. Leah, she told me she was proud of me, and I couldn't be more grateful of that. I will carry that with me always. Every time I think of Madisonville or go there, I will always think of Ms. Leah and be grateful for her.

HUNGARIAN STUFFED-CABBAGE ROLLS

MAKES 30 TO 40 CABBAGE ROLLS

2 to 3 heads cabbage, depending on size

2 tablespoons olive oil

1 onion, finely chopped

½ cup uncooked long-grain rice

4 cloves garlic, chopped

1 pound ground pork

1 pound ground beef

1 tablespoon Creole seasoning

1½ teaspoons kosher salt

¾ teaspoon black pepper

2 pounds sauerkraut, rinsed, drained, and squeezed dry

1 (28-ounce) can diced tomatoes, undrained

1 (6-ounce) can tomato paste

3 to 4 cups tomato juice, divided

4 strips hardwood-smoked bacon

There are two different methods for preparing the cabbage leaves for rolling. One is to core the cabbage and steam the whole heads until tender. The other is to freeze the raw heads of cabbage in advance. The leaves will soften as they defrost, eliminating the need for steaming. The freezer method is much easier, but you do need to plan two days ahead.

Prepare the Cabbage Using the Freezer Method

Rinse the heads of cabbage and peel away the 2 outermost leaves and discard them. Pat each head dry and wrap them tightly with plastic wrap. Place the wrapped heads in a freezer bag and freeze until solid, 12–18 hours. Allow at least 24 hours for the cabbages to defrost in the refrigerator. Be sure to place a shallow pan under them as they release a lot of water as they thaw.

Prepare the Cabbage Using the Steam Method

Remove the cores and 2 outermost leaves from each head of cabbage. Add 2–3 inches of water to a large pot fitted with a steaming rack. Bring the water to a boil and place a head or two of cabbage in the pot. Cover and steam for 12–15 minutes, or until the leaves are tender and pliable enough to separate and roll. It may be helpful to remove the cabbage midway through the cooking time, remove a few of the most tender outer leaves and return the head to the pot to finish cooking.

Assemble

Prepare the cabbage leaves for rolling by removing them from the heads, layer by layer. Set the leaves aside, blotting any excess moisture with a kitchen towel. Depending on the diameter of the cabbages, you will need 30 to 40 leaves to accommodate the quantity of meat in this recipe. Reserve the remaining cabbage for chopping.

Continued

To ensure easy rolling, slice off the thickest portion of the center vein of each cabbage leaf. Turn each leaf outer side up and insert the point of a paring knife just under the thinnest part of the center vein and slice toward the bottom of the leaf, being careful not to cut all the way through. This will help the vein from being so thick. Reserve the veins to be chopped and added to the cooking pot.

Heat the oil in a large pan over medium heat. Add the onion and sauté until soft and translucent, 3–5 minutes. Add the uncooked rice and stir until coated with oil. Continue cooking, stirring continually, for about 2 minutes, then add the garlic. Continue to sauté until the rice is lightly toasted and golden in color, 3–4 minutes more. Be sure to stir continuously to prevent the garlic from browning. Remove from the heat and set aside to cool for about 10 minutes.

Place the pork and beef in a large bowl. Add the Creole seasoning, salt, pepper, and the cooled onion-rice mixture. Using your hands, combine thoroughly, making sure that the seasonings and rice are evenly distributed throughout the meat.

To roll the cabbage, place a leaf, inner side up on a towel. Place 1½ to 2 tablespoons of the meat mixture at the bottom center of the leaf. Roll the cabbage leaf around the filling, using just enough pressure to make a firm roll without splitting the leaf. Using a paring knife, trim away the extra cabbage on the sides, leaving about ¾ inch of unfilled cabbage on either side for tucking in. Set aside the trimmings to be chopped and added to the cooking pot.

Using your thumb and middle finger on either side of the roll, gently tuck the ends of the cabbage into the meat mixture, forming a dimple on each end. Set the finished rolls aside as you work.

Once you've used up all of the meat, take what's left of the cabbage along with the trimmed veins and ends, chop them roughly, and place them in a very large bowl. Add the sauerkraut and mix well. Add the tomatoes, tomato paste, and 1 cup of the tomato juice. Combine thoroughly.

Preheat oven to 350 degrees. Coat a large pot or Dutch oven with nonstick spray.

Place a ¾-inch-thick layer of the cabbage, sauerkraut, and tomato mixture in the bottom. Layer some cabbage rolls on top, keeping them ½ inch or so from the sides of the pot. Add another, thinner layer of cabbage and tomato mixture, then more cabbage rolls, repeating as needed, finishing with a layer of the cabbage-tomato mixture.

Pour 2 cups of tomato juice evenly over the rolls and around the edges of the pot, making sure all the rolls are moistened, but not necessarily submerged in liquid. Lay the bacon strips over the top and cover tightly. Bake for 2 hours, checking midway through the cooking time to see if more tomato juice is needed to keep the rolls moist.

After 2 hours, test for doneness by cutting one of the cabbage rolls in half and tasting to see if the rice is tender. If not, return the pot to the oven for an additional 30–60 minutes.

NORTHSHORE CHICKEN AND MARKET VEGETABLE SALAD WITH PEPPER JELLY VINAIGRETTE

SERVES 6

5 Roma tomatoes, halved lengthwise

2 tablespoons vegetable oil

2 ears corn, shucked

6 (½-inch-thick) slices red onion

Cooking spray

1 pound boneless chicken breasts

2 tablespoons Creole seasoning

3 cups baby arugula

1 head Romaine lettuce, sliced into strips

Pepper Jelly Vinaigrette, divided

1 cup sliced English cucumber

2 cups cherry or grape tomatoes, halved

½ avocado, thinly sliced

⅓ cup basil leaves

Preheat oven to 350 degrees.

Toss Roma tomatoes in oil and arrange on a wire rack placed on a baking sheet. Roast 1 hour or until tomatoes are slightly browned and skins begin to pull away; let cool. Remove tomato skins and cut tomatoes in half horizontally, discarding skins.

Preheat grill pan on medium-high heat. Coat corn and red onion slices with cooking spray. Place in pan coated with cooking spray. Cook 12 minutes or until charred, turning occasionally. Remove from pan. Cut kernels from corn; discarding cobs.

Sprinkle chicken with Creole seasoning. Cook chicken in grill pan 12 minutes or until cooked through, turning occasionally; let stand 5 minutes. Thinly slice chicken across the grain.

Combine arugula and lettuce in a large bowl. Add 2 tablespoons vinaigrette; toss to coat. Top with cucumber, cherry tomatoes, red onion, chicken, corn, roasted tomato halves, and avocado. Sprinkle salad evenly with basil leaves, and serve with remaining dressing.

Continued

Pepper Jelly Vinaigrette

⅓ cup red wine vinegar

¼ cup vegetable oil

3 tablespoons red pepper jelly

1 small shallot, minced

1 teaspoon Creole mustard

¼ teaspoon kosher salt

¼ teaspoon ground black pepper

Place all ingredients in a medium bowl and whisk well.

SAVORY TERRINE

24 thick bacon slices, divided

2 boneless and skinless duck breasts

2 boneless and skinless chicken breasts

4 cups ground pork

2/3 cup heavy cream

3 tablespoons brandy

½ teaspoon black peppercorns, crushed

Kosher salt

1 bunch flat-leaf parsley, leaves picked

½ cup pistachios

½ cup dried cranberries

Serve with

Buttered toasted sourdough bread

Cornichons

Pickled onions

Dijon mustard

Caramelized onion chutney

Put slices of bacon onto a chopping board and use the back of a large knife to scrape and stretch out the bacon. Do this for each slice. Use 20 slices to line the bottom and sides of a 2-pound loaf pan, overlapping slightly and ensuring there is a little overhang.

Butterfly the duck and chicken breasts then halve so you have 2 flat, thin pieces of each breast. Mix the pork, cream, brandy, and black pepper in a bowl and season with salt. Check the seasoning by frying a little of the mix and tasting it—add more salt or pepper if you think it needs it.

Preheat oven to 325 degrees.

Start by adding a layer of pork mixture to the bacon-lined terrine, and then chicken breast pieces, a layer of parsley leaves, and a handful of pistachios and cranberries. Then the duck breast pieces, more pistachios, and cranberries. Finish with the pork mince.

Lay a few more slices of bacon along the central part of the terrine, and fold in all of the overhang. The terrine should be completely enclosed by the bacon. Wrap the top in a double layer of aluminum foil and bake in the oven for 1 hour.

Remove from the oven, allow to cool slightly, and pour off any fat. Cut a piece of cardboard so it fits snugly inside the pan on top of the terrine and wrap it in foil. Use the cardboard as a lid, and top with several cans to weigh the terrine down as it cools—this will give the terrine a tight, firm texture. Once cool, chill overnight, still weighted down. Slice and serve with toast, cornichons, pickled onions, mustard, and onion chutney.

ST. BERNARD PARISH
New Orleans' Most Historic Neighbor

When you say "Da Parish" most everyone knows you are talking about St. Bernard Parish, which is just five miles from the French Quarter, the heart of New Orleans. St. Bernard was settled in 1778 by Canary Islanders known as Isleños. We can thank the Isleños for the mirliton. "We know from ship manifests that they brought the chayote, or mirliton, to Louisiana," said Bill Hyland, official St. Bernard Parish Historian. This vegetable is widely grown and used in all of Louisiana. You will see it first hand in a recipe in this chapter as I show off my mom's stuffed mirliton, which I make regularly in my home. I have often said that mirliton is the tofu of squashes, because mirliton will take on the flavor of whatever you cook it with, and in countless ways. You can also eat it raw.

Just as our cooking draws so much from French cuisine, the Isleños drew from the Spanish but also Portuguese and North African flavor profiles. That is what I most love about the Isleños history of Louisiana. People have always migrated, celebrated, and were grateful for what was here, and brought their culture and flavors to create something new. That is the essence of Creole culture, and you can clearly see that in Da Parish.

BACON, CORN, AND SHRIMP CHOWDER

MAKES 6 SERVINGS

6 slices thick bacon, cut into ½-inch pieces

1 tablespoon butter

1 cup sliced green onions, divided

½ cup diced celery

4 cloves garlic, minced

1 tablespoon Creole seasoning

½ teaspoon kosher salt

¼ teaspoon black pepper

2 tablespoons all-purpose flour

2⅔ cups milk

1½ cups fresh or frozen corn kernels

1 (15-ounce) can creamed corn

¼ teaspoon cayenne pepper, plus more to taste

1 pound shrimp, peeled and deveined

1 teaspoon chopped thyme

⅓ cup half-and-half

Hot sauce

Cook the bacon in a Dutch oven over medium heat until crisp, about 6 minutes. With a slotted spoon, remove the bacon from the pan and transfer to a paper towel–lined plate. Lightly pat dry and set aside for serving. Discard all but 1 tablespoon bacon fat.

Add the butter to the bacon fat in the pot and let it melt. Set aside ¼ cup of the green onions for serving then add the rest of the green onions and celery to the pan. Cook, stirring occasionally, until the veggies are tender, about 3 minutes, then stir in the garlic, Creole seasoning, salt, and pepper. Cook until the garlic is fragrant, about 30 seconds.

Sprinkle the flour over the top of the onion mixture then cook, stirring constantly, for 1 minute. Slowly pour in the milk, a few splashes at a time at first, stirring out any lumps. Stream in the rest of the milk then add the corn kernels, creamed corn, and cayenne. Stir and bring to a gentle boil. Let bubble until thickened, about 5 minutes. Stir in the shrimp and continue cooking just until the shrimp are done, about 3 minutes. Remove from the heat then stir in the thyme and half-and-half. Serve hot, sprinkled with reserved bacon, green onions, and a dash or 2 of hot sauce as desired.

STUFFED MIRLITON

MAKES 6 TO 8 SERVINGS

6 mirliton (chayotes)

2 tablespoons butter

2 tablespoons vegetable oil

2 cups chopped onions

¼ cup sliced green onions

½ cup chopped green bell pepper

2 tablespoons Creole seasoning

4 cloves garlic, minced

1½ cups seasoned breadcrumbs, divided

1 teaspoon basil

½ teaspoon thyme

1 tablespoon hot sauce

Kosher salt and pepper to taste

1 pound shrimp, chopped

½ pound boiled ham, chopped

1 egg

4 tablespoons butter

Preheat oven to 350 degrees. Boil whole mirlitons in a pot of water until fork tender. Remove mirlitons from water and let cool.

Melt butter in a heavy pan and add oil. Add onions, green onions, and bell pepper and fry until soft. Add Creole seasoning and garlic in the last few minutes. Cut mirlitons in half and remove the large seed in center. Carefully scoop out pulp. Leave the shells of the mirlitons about ½ inch thick; set aside. Add pulp to onions and green pepper mixture; cook for about 15 minutes over medium heat.

Add 1 cup of breadcrumbs, basil, thyme, hot sauce, salt, and pepper. Add shrimp and ham and cook for 5 additional minutes. Add egg and stir until thoroughly blended into the mixture. Fill shells with mixture and sprinkle with remaining breadcrumbs. Dot with butter and bake until breadcrumbs are browned, about 20 minutes.

HUMMINGBIRD CAKE

2 cups pecans, chopped, divided

3 cups all-purpose flour

1 teaspoon baking soda

1½ teaspoons ground cinnamon

½ teaspoon allspice

½ teaspoon kosher salt

2 cups mashed bananas

1 (8-ounce) can crushed pineapple, drained

3 large eggs, room temperature

⅔ cup vegetable oil

1 cup packed dark brown sugar

¾ cup sugar

2 teaspoons vanilla extract

Cream Cheese Frosting

16 ounces cream cheese, softened

¾ cup butter, softened

5 cups powdered sugar

2 teaspoons vanilla extract

1 tablespoon milk

⅛ teaspoon salt, plus more to taste

Preheat oven to 300 degrees. Spread pecans onto a baking pan lined with parchment paper. Toast for 8 minutes. Remove from the oven. Turn oven up to 350 degrees then grease and lightly flour 3 (9-inch) cake pans.

Whisk the flour, baking soda, cinnamon, allspice, and salt together in a large bowl. Combine the bananas, pineapple, eggs, oil, brown sugar, sugar, and vanilla in a medium bowl. Pour wet ingredients into dry ingredients and stir until completely combined. Fold in 1½ cups toasted pecans.

Spread batter evenly between the prepared cake pans. Bake for 25–30 minutes or until a toothpick inserted in the center comes out clean. Rotate pans halfway through baking.

Remove cakes from the oven and allow to cool completely in the pans set on a wire rack. Once completely cooled, remove cakes from pans and level the tops off so they are flat.

To make frosting, use a hand or stand mixer to beat the cream cheese and butter together in a large bowl until smooth and creamy. Add powdered sugar, vanilla, milk, and salt. Beat on low speed for 30 seconds then switch to high speed and beat for 2 minutes. Taste. Add more salt if needed.

Place 1 cake layer on a cake stand or serving plate. Evenly cover the top with frosting. Top with second layer and evenly cover the top with frosting. Finish with the third cake layer and spread the remaining frosting all over the top and sides. Garnish with remaining toasted pecans. Refrigerate for at least 30 minutes before slicing or else the cake may fall apart as you cut.

NEW ORLEANS
Cookin' in the Crescent City

Louisiana is special, and when you mention Louisiana, more often than not, what people think about is New Orleans. New Orleans is home to me. New Orleans is where I was born, it's where I grew up, and it's where I raised my children. One of my most recent memories I would like to share is about Monica. Monica and I met in New Orleans over 20 years ago, and from day one there was something special. But when you love something, you let it go and see if it will come back to you. She came back to me. I proposed to Monica here in New Orleans. We found out that getting married can be difficult, expensive, and no one agrees on how to get married. Monica wanted to elope, I wanted my children and grandchildren there, and certain people wanted us to have a big wedding, and half-jokingly wanted us to rent out the Super Dome to get married.

We had been engaged for eighteen months, and had made no meaningful headway to getting married. It took me going to France for ten days

and being away from her to make me want to get married as soon as possible. I remember calling Monica and just saying, "Please marry me by the end of the year." And she said, "That's in two months, and we haven't made any progress towards getting married at all." She must have known I was serious because when we talked the next day, she asked me, "What about a surprise wedding?" It took me about a second to say "YES." And she was prepared with a plan.

The plan was to ask for help from some really important people at WYES-TV where my TV shows have been filmed. Earlier that fall, we had finished filming my latest TV show, *Kevin Belton's New Orleans Celebrations*. While I was in France, Monica and I finished editing my last cookbook. Monica suggested we organize a "celebration" celebrating the completion of a great year finishing my TV show and companion book. We talked to Allan Pizzato, the president of WYES and asked if he would loan us the facility. He said yes. Once we had the place, we asked a handful of people for help, and they would be the only people in the "know." Tam Kady, the Director of Production and Event Services at WYES helped us organize everything and was our right-hand woman. Our really good friend (and my fishing buddy) Lenny Delbert, filmed the event for us. His son Lenny Delbert Jr, (who coincidently has the same birthday as I do, and now has the same wedding anniversary as well) did the lighting for us. Both Lennys have also been on the crews of my shows and have become family. Our good friend Eric Paulsen, anchor for WWL-TV in New Orleans, is licensed to marry people, and he flew back early from his Christmas break to "emcee our event" but actually to marry us. Everyone kept our secret for two long months.

We got a cake, but at the time that we ordered it, we had no idea what flavor it was or how it was going to be decorated. We got a friend and fellow chef to cook, and honestly, we had no idea what he was gonna cook. All we knew was that there was going to be food there. None of the specifics were important to us. What was important was that we were gonna get married on December 29, and that is exactly what happened.

It was a magical night where we were surrounded by eighty-five people who we know and love. We had an hour of cocktails and then the doors were opened to the very studio where I filmed *Kevin Belton's New Orleans Celebrations*. As people we finding a seat, Monica put on her wedding dress. And Eric Paulsen started the festivities. As he spoke, he asked our friend Don Vappie to play a song. Don strummed the Train song "Marry Me." Our guests were totally confused, but then Monica walked out in her wedding dress escorted by our little guy Noah. I think the screams and excitement might have been heard miles away. Not even my children knew we were getting married. And Eric married us. We didn't want any of the formalities that go along with getting married, we didn't want gifts or showers or anything of that nature, we just wanted to be married. And we got married with the help of a handful of friends who are so special to us. We got married in place that means so much to me, WYES in New Orleans. And that is yet another reason why New Orleans in Louisiana is so special to me.

LYONNAISE POTATOES

MAKES 4 SERVINGS

3 large baking potatoes

6 tablespoons butter, divided

2 onions, sliced

1 tablespoon kosher salt, divided

1 teaspoon ground black pepper, divided

¼ cup flat-leafed parsley, chopped

Preheat oven to 400 degrees. Par-cook potatoes by piercing each several times with a fork or knife tip and bake until tender, about 45 minutes. Allow potatoes to cool slightly.

Peel the potatoes, if desired, cut in half lengthwise, then cut each half into ¼-inch slices. Set aside.

In a large skillet over medium-high heat, heat 3 tablespoons of butter until melted. Add half of the potatoes and sauté until light brown, 4–5 minutes. Add half of the onions and a little salt and pepper, then continue cooking until potatoes are a golden brown and onions are just cooked through, 7–8 minutes. Remove from pan and set aside to keep warm. Repeat the process with the remaining butter, potatoes, onions, salt, and pepper.

When all potatoes and onions are cooked, toss with the parsley and serve immediately.

BOUDIN-STUFFED PORK CHOPS WITH CREOLE MUSTARD-CANE SYRUP GLAZE

MAKES 4 SERVINGS

2 cups boudin

1 egg, beaten

4 thick-cut pork chops

Creole seasoning to taste

2 tablespoons cooking oil

1 teaspoon kosher salt

½ teaspoon cayenne pepper

Creole Mustard-Cane Syrup Glaze

Preheat oven to 350 degrees.

Mix the boudin well with the egg. Cut a pocket into the side of each pork chop, coming about ½ inch from going through the other side. Season inside the pocket with Creole seasoning.

Stuff about ½ cup boudin into each chop, or as much as you can fit in without over stuffing it. Brush the chops with oil and season the outside liberally with Creole seasoning, salt, and cayenne.

Heat a cast iron skillet over medium high. Sear chops on both sides until nicely browned. Finish in the oven until just cooked through and the boudin is hot, about 15–20 minutes. Brush with the glaze and serve with your favorite sides.

Creole Mustard-Cane Syrup Glaze

MAKES 1/3 CUP

4 tablespoons Creole mustard

2 tablespoons cane syrup

1 spritz lemon juice

½ teaspoon kosher salt

½ teaspoon white pepper

Mix all ingredients together in a small bowl.

Boudin

MAKES 16 CUPS

3 cups short-grain rice, cooked and cooled

2 pounds pork shoulder, cut into 1-inch cubes

1 pound pork liver, cleaned and cut into large chunks

2 quarts chicken stock

1½ cups chopped onions

½ cup chopped green bell pepper

½ cup chopped celery

2 cloves garlic

2 teaspoons kosher salt, divided

2 tablespoons Creole seasoning, divided

2 teaspoons cayenne pepper, divided

1¼ teaspoons black pepper, divided

1 cup chopped parsley, divided

1 cup chopped green onions, divided

In a large bowl, add rice and fluff with a fork.

In a large Dutch oven, combine pork, liver, stock, onions, bell pepper, celery, garlic, 1 teaspoon salt, 1 tablespoon Creole seasoning, ¼ teaspoon cayenne, and ½ teaspoon black pepper. Bring to a boil over high heat; reduce heat to medium low, and simmer, uncovered, until pork and liver are tender, about 1½ hours. Remove from heat, and drain, reserving 1½ cups of broth.

In a meat grinder fitted with a ¼-inch dye, grind pork and liver with ¼ cup parsley and ¼ cup green onion. (The pork and liver can also be coarsely chopped, in batches, in the bowl of a food processor.)

In the large bowl, combine pork mixture and rice, and the remaining salt, Creole seasoning, cayenne, black pepper, parsley, and green onion. Mix well. Add reserved broth, about ½ cup at a time, combining until mixture is moist but holds together when squeezed.

Form mixture into balls or patties and use, or freeze for up to 3 months.

SHRIMP SCAMPI RISOTTO

Risotto

5 to 6 cups chicken stock

3 tablespoons olive oil

½ cup chopped shallots

2 cloves garlic, minced

1 cup Arborio rice

½ cup dry white wine

4 tablespoons butter

⅔ cup grated Parmesan cheese

Kosher salt and pepper, to taste

Shrimp Scampi

2 tablespoons olive oil

3 tablespoons butter

½ to 1 teaspoon red pepper flakes

½ onion, diced

4 cloves garlic, minced

1 pound shrimp, peeled and deveined

½ cup dry white wine

2 lemons, juiced

1 teaspoon kosher salt

½ teaspoon white pepper

Parsley, for garnish

Risotto

Make the risotto first; the shrimp will not take long to cook.

Heat stock in saucepan over medium heat; keep at a low simmer. Heat oil in a heavy-bottom saucepan over medium heat. Add shallots to oil, and cook, stirring, until translucent. Add garlic and cook for 1 additional minute. Add rice, and cook, stirring, until rice begins to make a clicking sound like glass beads, 3-4 minutes. Add wine to rice mixture. Cook, stirring, until wine is absorbed by rice.

Using a ladle, add ¾ cup hot stock to rice. Using a wooden spoon, stir rice constantly, at a moderate speed. When rice mixture is just thick enough to leave a clear wake behind the spoon, add another ¾ cup stock.

Continue adding stock, ¾ cup at a time, and stirring constantly until rice is mostly translucent but still opaque in the center. Rice should be al dente but not crunchy. As rice nears doneness, watch carefully and add smaller amounts of liquid to make sure it does not overcook. The final mixture should be thick enough that grains of rice are suspended in liquid the consistency of heavy cream. It will thicken slightly when removed from heat.

Remove from heat. Stir in butter and Parmesan cheese. Season with salt and pepper. Divide into serving bowls, and top with shrimp scampi.

Shrimp Scampi

Heat oil, butter and red pepper flakes in large skillet over medium heat. Add onion and cook for 2-3 minutes, or until onion is translucent. Add garlic and cook for 1 additional minute.

Increase heat to high, and add in the shrimp in a single layer. Add wine, lemon juice, salt, and pepper and cook for 2-3 minutes. Flip shrimp and cook for an additional 1-2 minutes until the shrimp are pink and opaque. Remove from heat and garnish with parsley. Serve with risotto.

GLOSSARY

and Guide to Knowing, Loving, and Understanding Louisiana

Acadians (uh-KAY-dee-enz)—descendants of Nova Scotia who settled in Louisiana in the eighteenth century. Later shortened to Cajun, which became synonymous with the food, music, and culture of the Acadian people.

Amandine (AH-mahn-deen)—fish or seafood served with a topping of lemon, butter, and slivered almonds.

Andouille (AHN-do-ee)—a seasoned smoked country sausage used in gumbo and other dishes.

Bayou (BY-you)—a small river or stream with a slow current.

Beignets (ben-YEYZ)—square donuts covered with powdered sugar, often served with café au lait or hot chocolate.

Bisque (bisk)—a thick, cream-, milk- or tomato-based shellfish soup usually made with crawfish, shrimp, crab, or oysters.

Boucherie (BOO-shuh-ree)—a community butchering which involves several families contributing the animals, usually pigs, to be slaughtered. Each family gets a share of the butchering. This was traditionally done in the late fall to provide meat during winter.

Boudin (BOO-dan)—a Cajun sausage filled with seasoned meat and rice.

Ca c'est bon (Sa say bohn)—that's good.

Café au lait—coffee with milk.

Cajun (kay-jun)—French Acadians who settled here after immigrating from Canada.

Calliope—a musical instrument found on steamboats consisting of a set of steam whistles played from a keyboard.

Cane syrup—rich, sweet syrup extracted from sugar cane.

Cher (share)—Cajun word for dear.

Chicory (CHIK-uh-ree)—the roots of endive which are dried, ground, roasted, and used to flavor coffee.

Cochon de lait (KO-shon duh-LAY)—the roasting of a suckling pig over an open fire until the inside is cooked tender and the outside is bacon-like.

Crawfish—a freshwater shellfish resembling a miniature lobster eaten in étouffée, jambalaya, gumbos, or boiled with spices. Sometimes called mudbugs.

Creole (KREE-ol)—descendants of French, Spanish, and Caribbean peoples. Can refer to a people or a style of cooking, music, or architecture.

Da Parish—Chalmette, a suburb of New Orleans.

Dressed—when you order a po'boy "dressed" which means you want lettuce, tomatoes, pickles, and mayo on it.

Envie (ah n vee)—a longing or hunger to do or eat something.

Fais do-do (Fay' dough dough)—a Cajun dance party, after the children have gone to sleep.

Filé (FEE-lay)—ground sassafras leaves used to season and thicken gumbo.

GNO—Greater New Orleans area.

Gratons (grat-TOHNZ)—Cajun word for cracklings or deep-fried pig skins.

Gris-Gris (gree-gree)—to put a curse on someone. Often used in jest, not in reference to black magic.

Grillades (GRIH-ahdz)—beef or veal round steak simmered in a browned tomato sauce and served over rice or grits.

Gumbo (GUM-bo)—thick, seasoned soup prepared with ingredients such as sausage, chicken, seafood and okra and served over rice.

Gumbo Ya Ya—everybody talking at once.

Hurricane party—what some New Orleanians do after securing their houses for a hurricane: throw a party! (If it's safe to stay, that is!) Get some snacks, drinks, and friends and hunker down to watch the TV news give hurricane updates. Hurricane is also the name of a famous New Orleans drink. Be careful because they are strong and will catch up to you.

Hush Puppies—deep-fried cornbread balls.

Joie de vivre (JWAH-duh-veev)—a joyous attitude toward life.

King cake—a ring-shaped oval cake decorated with glaze and colored sugar in the traditional Mardi Gras colors purple, green, and gold, which represent justice, faith, and power. A small plastic baby is hidden inside the cake. Tradition requires that the person who gets the cake slice hiding the baby buys or makes the next gathering's cake.

Krewe (crew)—a Mardi Gras organization's members.

Lagniappe (lan-yap)—a Cajun-French inspired noun that means "a little extra." Receiving anything extra and better yet, receiving something for free.

Laissez les bon temps rouler—let the good times roll.

Levee (LEV-ee)—an embankment built to keep a river, or lake from overflowing.

Lundi Gras—the day before Mardi Gras, when King Rex and King Zulu arrive on the riverfront.

Makin groceries—buying groceries.

Mardi Gras (MAR-dee graw)—commonly known as "Fat Tuesday" or Carnival. It is the day before Ash Wednesday, which is the first day of the Lenten season in the Catholic Church.

Mirliton—chayote squash.

Muffuletta (Moo Fa' lotta)—large, round, fat sandwich filled with salami-type meats, mozzarella cheese, pickles, and olive salad.

Neutral ground—median or grassy area between the paved areas on a boulevard. Named for the original Canal St. division between the Americans and Creoles, who did not like each other.

Okra (OH-kruh)—a vegetable used to flavor and thicken gumbo, or served as a side dish.

Parish—Louisiana has parishes, not counties.

Po'boy—or poor boy, a long sandwich on French bread usually stuffed with oysters, shrimp, or roast beef. South Louisiana version of a submarine or hero sandwich.

Praline (prah-LEEN)—a candy made of white and brown sugar, milk, butter, and pecans.

Repass—the meal and gathering after a funeral.

Roux (ROO)—flour and oil or butter cooked to a spectrum from a blond roux all the way to a black roux and used to start many Louisiana dishes.

Rue (ROO)—the French word for street.

Sauce Piquante (pee-KAWNT)—thick, sharp sauce made with roux and tomatoes that is highly seasoned with herbs and peppers and simmered for hours.

Second line—a celebratory dance accompanied by jazz and decorated umbrellas; a south Louisiana tradition at weddings, jazz funerals, and other festive occasions.

Shotgun—a single row house in which all rooms on one side are connected by a long single hallway—you can open the front door and shoot a gun straight through the back door, without hitting a single wall.

Snoball (not spelled snowball)—shaved ice which resembles powder, served with flavored syrup poured over it.

Swamp—a low, freshwater wetland that is heavily forested and subject to seasonal flooding.

Tasso (TAH-so)—seasoned pork pieces that are smoked and used to flavor dishes.

Trinity—a mixture of onions, celery, and bell peppers used in Cajun and Creole cuisine.

"Throw Me Something, Mister!"—What everyone yells at parades to get throws from the maskers on the floats!

Twinspan—The twin bridges connecting the North Shore at Slidell with New Orleans across Lake Pontchartrain.

Vieux Carre' (View ca ray')—French for "Old Square," a term used for the French Quarter.

Voodoo—Some consider Voodoo a religion, some a form of witchcraft, and some just spooky fun.

Where y'at?—this is how you say "How are you?"

Who dat?—A New Orleans Saints fan and a chant. "Who dat? Who dat? Who dat say dey gonna beat dem Saints?"

Zydeco (ZYE-duh-koe)—a music style from Southwest Louisiana, created by the French Creole people living there. It blends R&B, blues, jazz, and gospel with indigenous music from Creole and Native American peoples of Louisiana.

INDEX

METRIC CONVERSION CHART

Volume Measurements		Weight Measurements		Temperature Conversion	
U.S.	Metric	U.S.	Metric	Fahrenheit	Celsius
1 teaspoon	5 ml	½ ounce	15 g	250	120
1 tablespoon	15 ml	1 ounce	30 g	300	150
¼ cup	60 ml	3 ounces	90 g	325	160
⅓ cup	75 ml	4 ounces	115 g	350	180
½ cup	125 ml	8 ounces	225 g	375	190
⅔ cup	150 ml	12 ounces	350 g	400	200
¾ cup	175 ml	1 pound	450 g	425	220
1 cup	250 ml	2¼ pounds	1 kg	450	230